CREATE SOMETHING

CREATE SOMETHING

LILLY BENITEZ

CRAFTING AN ENTREPRENEURIAL JOURNEY

CREATE SOMETHING

CRAFTING AN ENTREPRENEURIAL JOURNEY

ISBN 9798989411214 paperback
ISBN 9798989411221 ebook
ISBN 9798989411207 hardcover

Cover Design by:
Wes Phelan
www.banowetz.com

Interior Design by:
Chris Treccani
www.3dogcreative.net

Table Of Contents

Dedicated to Papi and Mami as well as those
who have encouraged me along the way.

1:

FOLLOW YOUR OBSESSIONS

"I do have an obsessive personality, but striving for perfection has served me well."
- Tom Ford

There it was again: the storefront of the school, coming into focus as if I were driving up to it. The thrill and excitement of recognizing the place were palpable. It was a welcome surprise, yet also terrifying, before I awoke.

How many nights can one dream with such clarity that taking action no longer feels like a choice?

As a child, I endured a recurring dream of profound intensity. The same haunting scene would play out in my mind every few weeks. It always began in the bright daylight of a lush paradise with the humidity of a tropical climate. Pablo, my brother and earliest companion, and I would run through the dense foliage of flowers and deep greens, playing games and climbing without restraints. We would always make it home just as the sun was setting.

In this dream, we belonged to a community with cyclical evening rituals. As the darkness enveloped us, a clear, cooling light descended from the heavens. Chosen individuals - beloved family members, neighbors, and friends - would step into this ray of light. As we meditated in stillness, they would rise, vanishing into the heavenly light, each group different from the last.

Through a child's eyes, many things are accepted without question. Yet, this was different. It felt solemn, even desolate.

My father would hold me, calmly explaining that there would come a time for each of us to step into that light. Everyone's time was different, though. This wasn't a journey for families but instead an individual one. This experience was deeply personal, inevitable, and transcended origins.

Loving my father as deeply as I did, I remember trying to come up with loopholes and escape plans. He'd smile in that knowing way fathers do.

"No hay nada de qué preocuparse, es natural," he'd say.

"There is nothing to worry about; it is natural."

The days in my dream would shorten, the lights appearing more frequently until the day my Dad had to say goodbye. As he moved towards the light, I would rebel and rage in fear. He was my father, and he belonged to me.

This is when I would awaken, tears streaming. I would search for him all over the house, to my mother's dismay. She would try to comfort me in a world without cell phones, which weren't a thing in the late 80s, reminding me that he was at work and would be home soon. I would sit and wait for him by the window. The moment he pulled up in his crumbly truck, I would dash to hug him and squeeze him and tell him how much I loved him and beg him to please never go away.

Losing my father in reality, in a car accident in the same Montero that had transported us on our favorite expedition to El Salvador, made me extra wary of recurring dreams. That's why the dream of Blade Craft Barber Academy's facade was not exhilarating for me. On the contrary, it weighed heavily on my heart.

Over time, however, the dream transformed from an unsettling intruder to a comforting companion. The whispers in it grew louder until they solidified into an undeniable vision.

The generation before me arrived in the United States pursuing a calling for a better reality for themselves and their kin. Their stories and experiences are interlaced in my upbringing and result in my belief that following my own obsession to create an academy that indoctrinates a luxury level of barbering can become a reality.

Surely, my pursuit of a business providing a tangible and quantifiable product should yield delicious fruit. If my parents physically walked to the USA, fleeing civil war and child exploitation from three nations away, then surely creating a business that wasn't there would be easily attainable.

Clarity of vision is crucial. You cannot attain something you cannot envision. The movie in your mind's eye of how your business will look, feel, smell, and what emotions it will evoke must all be clear to you in the same way you can recount your favorite film or book. This process will help you understand the details that will become the final product.

Be intentional in that your efforts propel your calling or art form forward. Tomorrow is not promised, and time is fleeting. Act with intention through the discomfort of the unknown towards any momentum of making your goal a reality. If your dream is a product, create small batches of it and get feedback. If your dream is a service, offer it to friends and family while documenting the process diligently. Record the timing, cost, and supplies to create. Be intentional in that your calling stems from a need for the end result for a positive reason. Any time you spend making it happen can be fueled with intention, and you decide what that is.

The realm between nightmares and dreams can seem almost palpable. The most dreadful nightmare as a child of losing my favorite person transformed into a living reality, and yet I am still here despite the pain of tremendous loss. This is a story of action.

Diamonds In The Rough

- Your calling is something that pulls you towards "it."
- While the calling may seem like an obsession, the intention of the idea settles in your heart and mind for you to pursue it at all costs.
- Once the vision is clear, YOU must strive after the details of it until it becomes clear to others.
- Strive to make an effort to propel the future of your industry & generation forward to a more enriched state.

Discovery Questions

- How can you clarify the details of your dream and vision?
- Can you draw it or voice record the emotions they will feel?
- How can you envision the desired result daily?
- Remember that the vision you are seeing is merely the door or portal into THAT beginning!

Origen

Mami solía usar faldas largas llenas de diseños floridos con muchos colores, principalmente para honrar su religión pero también porque le servían para mil usos. Las usaba para secarse las manos, limpiar alguna que otra fruta o para cubrirse las piernas cuando tenía frío. Con ellas nos limpiaba el sudor de la cara, las lágrimas o mocos. Si se presentaba la ocasión, también las usaba para darnos privacidad cuando nos sentábamos entre sus pies para orinar afuera en los campos de El Salvador o durante los largos viajes en carro.

Mis primos y yo teníamos varias formas de divertirnos cuando nos ponían tareas. Los viajes a las tiendas que vendían gaseosas en bolsa, charamuscas y los benditos choco bananos prácticamente ameritaban que nos abrieran una cuenta sin fondo por ser clientes frecuentes. Nuestros favoritos eran las bolsas de canicas que venían surtidas con diferentes colores y texturas. Cada canica tenía un diseño único y

Origin

Mami's skirts were covered in colorful floral designs and, long to respect the religion, served a thousand purposes. It was the first thing she reached for to dry her hands, clean fruit, or stretch to cover her legs when she got cold. The skirt's underside wiped our faces from sweat, snot, and tears. When the opportunity presented itself, she would also use it to give us privacy when we squatted between her feet to urinate in the fields of El Salvador should the need arise on long road trips.

My cousins and I had many ways to entertain ourselves between chores. The street stores sold us sodas in plastic bags and charamuscas, and they should have just opened us a tab for the blessed choco bananos for being such frequent customers.

We sorted the bags of marbles with different textures and colors.

Each marble had a unique design, and the dirt allowed us to start games anew like an organic etch-a-sketch.

la textura de la tierra nos permitía jugar sin parar con facilidad. Los capiruchos y los trompos eran juguetes de madera muy entretenidos, pero nada se comparaba con la risa y la felicidad que le ocasionaba a mamá vernos jugar.

A nuestro tío Chungo, el de la espalda de guineo, le gustaba bailar para hacer reír a su hermana. Era el hermano soltero de mami, con rizos negros oscuros y siempre con una sonrisa de oreja a oreja, era una fiesta ambulante. No había oportunidad que dejara pasar para mover las caderas al ritmo de la música.

La tierra de mis padres siempre fue un lugar que les llamó por más que intentaban crear una vida e Dallas, El Salvador les corría por la sangre y cualquier excusa les bastaba para regresar.

The wooden stick with a cup toy and the spinning tops were entertaining, but nothing was as joyful as Mami's laughter. The banana-shaped back danced nonstop to make his sister laugh. Our uncle Chungo la Mona, Mami's bachelor brother, wore dark curls and smiled from ear to ear. He never wasted the opportunity to move his hips to and fro with the music as an ambulant party.

My parents always felt a calling from their native land despite creating a life in Dallas, and they always missed El Salvador. Any reason to return was enough.

2.

NOTICE NATURAL TALENTS

"When you start writing in a journal, commit to completing it front to back. Do not rip out a single page. As time passes, you will be able to look back at the challenges you overcame by simply reaching for one from a few years back."

-Al

How do I tell you this story? I will attempt to find a beginning.

As if by magic, my parents always found a way to have us spend our summers in El Salvador with their parents. God only knows how they engineered the feat each year with Papi working as a humble mechanic, carpenter, plumber, moonlighting as an electrician, or multi-purpose repairman, as long as it was honest work, and he could be home for dinner.

Mami made the most delicious homemade tacos. Pablo and I would help peel potatoes and package her spicy salsa that was too spicy, in my opinion, but the underdeveloped taste buds of a five-year-old don't have any pull in a business decision of that magnitude. The client was always right, and they loved it. We would drive up and sell them at junkyards and auto salvage shops.

The driveway of our home resembled a Pick-and-Pull itself with the dismantled trucks and cars Papi worked on in his free time. They were only the best: Datsun, Mitsubishi, Toyota, or Nissan, all imports. After being in the sun all day, he enjoyed the homemade dinner and took advantage of the barely cooler evening air by tinkering with the automobiles.

The white Mitsubishi Montero, frankensteined with a black hood, filled him with pride when the motor purred better and louder after a completely new install. It occurred to him that he would put his handy work to the test, and instead of flying to El Salvador, we could drive there in his project. We would save so much money, and we could even invite one of Mami's favorite brothers, Tio Nicho. He coaxed at her, sure it would pan out.

Papi excitedly poured over the imagery of all we would see on our journey. It was the Summer of 1995, and our family had grown to 5, with Noe, my baby brother, being born over a year prior. The more excited Papi got, the more Mami seemed convinced of the control we would have on the journey. Mami's usual saying, "*Pa luego es tarde,*" loosely means "the sooner the better."

But how would we navigate? El Salvador was three borders away from Dallas, TX.

How would we arrive?

How would we survive?

My parents decided I would be in charge of the map since I could translate from English to Spanish aloud with the same speed that I could read it. I was ten years old.

This process would later become how I outlined major projects and staked out solutions to obstacles in my life. You will draw from your personal story to create something that wasn't there because your strengths originate there. Seemingly mundane details all led to the materialization of my dream to start my own business by creating a barber academy with a culture to influence multitudes positively.

The strengths that have driven my will are informal, unrefined, and not exactly wanted. Being told that I was in charge of getting us to El Salvador at the age of ten felt similar to the news that writing a business plan was necessary to start a business. The asks felt too important, and I felt unprepared, but in both instances, I was willing!

The innocence of a child-like hope is a beautiful thing to remember and call on. How could I have known that all dreams aren't dreamy and that the immense pain in parts of the journey could all become beautiful?

Diamonds In The Rough

- If you are willing, adventures are calling.
- Notice your natural talents.

Discovery Questions

- What are the top three stories about yourself in which you demonstrated qualities that you admire?
- What are the qualities?
- How can you continue to develop them?

Mochila Y Valijas Llenas

Al darme cuenta que el sueño de irnos a El Salvador por tierra era una posibilidad real, lo primero que hice fue llamar a mi amiga Katrina para comentárselo y se lo contó con tanta alegría a su mamá, Janice.

Janice siempre había sido muy generosa conmigo, me mandaba postres con Katrina a la escuela y siempre estaba ahí para escucharme y me comprendía en momentos en los que quizá otro adulto no podría. Un día de sorpresa, me regaló una mochila llena de libros usados para que tuviese algo para leer durante el camino de nuestro viaje. Desde ese momento siempre he mantenido la costumbre de viajar con al menos un libro.

Mami nos pidió que llenáramos las valijas con toda la ropa que ya no nos quedaba, pues toditita se tendría que quedar allá. Nuestros primos y los niños de El Salvador, la necesitan más que nosotros y llenos de entusiasmo nos sentábamos encima de las bolsas para que cerrasen.

A Backpack and Full Luggage

Once I realized that the dream of traveling to El Salvador by land was a real possibility, I ran to call my friend Katrina, who excitedly shared the news with her mother, Janice.

Janice had always been very generous and kind to me, sending extra desserts in Katrina's lunch for her to share. She had always listened to me like a person and understood me in ways that other adults in my life couldn't. To my surprise, one day, she gifted me a backpack full of used books so I might have something to read on the international road trip. Since that moment, I have always maintained the habit of traveling with a book.

Our suitcases were filled to the brim and all of the clothes would have to stay in El Salvador on our return. Mami had us pack the clothes that currently fit us or we had grown out of. We sat on the suitcases with the enthusiasm that comes from the knowledge that others would benefit from them.

3.

ADDRESS AN EXISTING NEED

*"Visualization works if you work hard. That's the thing.
You can't just visualize and go eat a sandwich."*
-Jim Carrey

On the journey to create something that wasn't there, necessity is a helpful friend on "what" that something could be. I enjoyed barbering and caring for my Regulars when I could no longer ignore the "something."

The straight razor gleamed as she carefully closed it and set it on the counter. Marcella balled up her hands into fists, shaky and angry. She yelled at me through teary eyes that she wasn't prepared. Stomping her feet and emotional, she expressed I was too hard on her and that it wasn't fair.

Marcella had completed 300 hours at a Barber School in Texas to prepare her for 85 questions on a Written Exam covering diverse subjects with terminology on microbiology and chemistry as it relates to the skin and hair. The textbook had never been addressed during her time of training. Her reading was at a 5th-grade level, coupled with Dyslexia.

There was also a timed Practical Exam scrutinizing various technical skills such as a haircut, straight razor shave, and facial, all within a 3-hour and 29-minute timeframe. The instructors never introduced it, much less reviewed it with her in that so-called"-school."

Marcella's livelihood was now in jeopardy since our boss had paid for her training. The company expected the diversity in its services to generate more traction and added revenue. She kept avoiding scheduling the exams, and our boss had now asked me to intervene and get her licensed because she was obviously nowhere ready to pass.

I was busy barbering, and people kept asking me, "When will you open your own place?" The loyalty of my clientele throughout the years meant they saw me go through varied stages of growth. My eagerness to care for them and my passion for barbering led them to ask me when I planned to do my own thing, especially after obtaining my instructor license.

The process I had taken to become a massage therapist, barber, and then an educator was unique to most of my clientele in that most of them had gone through traditional four-year Universities and beyond. As they heard of my trade acquisitions, we often discussed how different their studies at college had been from my vocational programs.

As flattering as their belief in me seemed, the real question was how would I staff a place of my own? Marcella's experience was not an anomaly. Graduates were not prepared in the specifics of service, technical ability, and entrepreneurial skills. I would be in the same predicament as all the barbering businesses I had been part of.

The level of training and practice is on display when exhaustion, stress, or volume push us to our limits. . Education is the foundation of long-term success in our trade because it is immediately actionable, timeless, and a source of deep connection between the barber and fellow man.

I found my callings through the necessity of helping others. I honed my skills by pursuing my calling and devising a plan to overcome each obstacle. I created a personalized training in which Marcella and I worked together for three weeks. She completed assignments at home at her pace instead of reading aloud to me in person and passed the Written Exam.

To prevent her hands from shaking on the straight razor shave, I demonstrated the strokes with a bladed razor, and she followed me with a nonloaded razor. I developed an array of exercises to remove the fear or danger of the razor by providing guidance with companionship. She hugged me, beaming with pride when she passed her last exam with flying colors. Almost a decade later, she now leads a staff and business in which she provides the highest level of luxury barbering.

Marcella's need created the opportunity for the skills I had been honing to answer the question of what I needed to develop that wasn't there to elevate the barbering industry. I truly believed I could offer guidance to provide a barbering experience unlike any other, but I needed clarity on the how.

Diamonds In The Rough

- The calling of an obsession towards achieving a goal or materializing an intangible dream fuels the pursuit. Action, however, is required.

Discovery Questions

- What is a need in your industry or product offering?
- What is a service you could offer that would add value to others?
- What are similar services priced in other sectors ?

El Mapa

Y fue así que con un mapa de Tejas que compramos en la gasolinera partimos rumbo a El Salvador.

"Veremos si es verdad que has estudiado" me amenazaba Mami. "Usted está encargada de guiarnos todo el camino, usted es una niña inteligente" me decía Papi. "Con Dios mediante llegaremos bien."

Papi iba al volante, cada uno en su lugar y yo siguiendo el mapa.

The Map

And this was how, with a gas station-bought map of Texas, we parted towards El Salvador.

"We shall see if you have really been studying," threatened Mami. "You are in charge of guiding us correctly through our journey in that you are an intelligent girl."

Papi handled the steering wheel, everyone was in their seat, and I followed the map.

4.
SOLVE YOUR OWN PROBLEMS

*"Go confidently in the direction of your dreams!
Live the life you've imagined."*
-Henry David Thoreau

While only a happy barber, I had the opportunity to travel for a skincare product line and support its sales and influence. During this time, I always visited various barbershops in the cities I had stops in and met with barbers who offered shaving as a service.

In my travels, I realized that the skill of the straight razor shave was rare and training for it didn't really exist. Not to mention, the escape or the experience that was the actual service I was providing back home was not happening anywhere I traveled. How could I create an educational experience that ensured connection through relaxation?

Since 2008, we have become more aware that the importance of a healthy option for a third place was long overdue. Men had the home as first, their work as second, and the spaces they regularly frequented in between were considered third place. With the convenience of the internet, bars and strip clubs still left something lacking. Men didn't consider them to have as great allure as generations prior. People were looking to be heard, making in-person connections that much more critical.

Unique barber lifestyle clubs were creating a dent in that gap, and a barbershop offered all of these experiences simultaneously, in addition to networking opportunities with like-minded people.

Barbershops were churches for bad people, a holy ground where all denominations, sexual orientations, and political spectrums could be brethren at the fragrant lather-filled hands of the barber.

I had no idea where to begin planning for the creation of the academy or to refine my barbering experience possibilities further. The need for the third place clarified that to fulfill the demand, training for barbers would need to be available. In pursuing the clarity of my goal, it was clear the idea needed to be broken down in detail to ensure Marcella's experience was no more.

Crazy curly hair Charm was an extremely talented hairdresser who served the Dallas elite, had editorial experience, and was kind enough to share his favorite contacts in New York. His salon was an exceptionally fun place to work, and during my time with him, he offered more than his two cents on business creation. He told me the harsh reality that if I wanted to be taken seriously, I needed to write a business plan. As gross as it sounded for a creative person to write a business plan, his advice proved right for me.

I booked a flight to NY and toured all of the unique barber shops he mentioned, plus salon education spots as well. Marcella's unimpressive barbering educational experience was not an anomaly in our state, and it was an issue nationwide.

I needed to write a business plan. Gross.

A friend heard of my strife and printed a MASSIVE binder full of SBA resources for me to refer to during my new unwelcome assignment. No matter how much I wrote, the insecurity that the plan wasn't adding up meant that I needed more applicable assistance. Projections were daunting because they were imaginary numbers that I was supposed to somehow leverage to obtain capital.

How could I execute on the advice of writing my business plan with no prior experience, and how could I condense it into simple, actionable terms? In seeking guidance, my assumption was to trust degrees and titles until I lost income because of it.

I searched reviews and found a Business Consultant. He required a week's worth of my income in retainer, which I knew had to be a worthy investment. It only resulted in unanswered calls and a lack of guidance. I was overwhelmed.

I felt disillusioned and disheartened. I decided that Starting a Business course at SMU for eight weeks could maybe steer me and get the crazy idea out of my mind. I knew I didn't traditionally belong in a course with those obtaining Master and Doctorate-level Business degrees, but I'd try it.

The first day of class arrived. After dealing with finding the correct building and parking, I felt a wave of anxiety wash over me. What was I thinking? I didn't go here. I wasn't a college person. What possessed me to just sign myself up like that?!

I walked towards the hall after asking for directions, and there on the wall were elegant frames housing the pictures of some of the most decorated Donors and Alumni. As I scanned through the faces, I felt connection and recognition in a set of eyes. A familiar smile and gaze met me there in the ocean of portraits. There to greet me from decades past was none other than Al. Al had been one of my regulars that shared his entrepreneurship journey and gave me countless WOW (words of wisdom) throughout his barbering visits.

I did belong here. Here was where I was supposed to be.

The door to the class was heavy, light-toned wood, and the handle was cool to the touch. I was in and smiled, knowing this would be something special, and I couldn't wait to tell Al at his next appointment! He'd be so proud.

I'd learn to write this plan even if it terrified me.

My Starting a Business Class at SMU was taught by Jerry, a man with a knack for speaking. While there were terms I had never heard and businesses on topics I didn't know were a thing, moments of clarity appeared & convinced me I was on the right track.

He mentioned that if you didn't have experience working in the business you were trying to create, it was imperative that you obtain it before investing in it. He also stated that cash flow is the number one issue a company must address. Cash flow is different from profit. A business without cash flow is dead.

This advice has always stuck with me in that we tend to romanticize the idea of going off on our own and beginning things our way. Money is part of that becoming a reality. Cash flow doesn't initiate the warm fuzzies, but it's a good thing that we can learn to love, especially if pursuing that love leads to the survival of our initial idea.

Accounting doesn't seem sexy, but living life on your terms is. All tangible dreams have aspects that aren't why you start but must be addressed to provide lifeblood to your calling. You will find a way to push past the discomfort, though, because the purpose of what you are doing is greater than the temporary discomfort.

After being seated for a while, a happy woman with bright, fuschia-colored hair introduced herself to me as Julia. Oh, the joy! Another creative in the same class as me! She had a business where she took trash or unwanted things and turned them into art! Her energy and excitement were contagious, and we became fast friends. We managed to save each other's seats and tried to lessen the confusion of the Venture Capitalist terms being thrown around when addressing how to conduct business in China.

Through this friendship, she let me know of her friend Myrtle, a retiree with a couple of antique barber items. Myrtle and her husband were in their late 80s and were very particular about who they would be willing to sell them to. I had some savings to create Blade Craft. I figured visiting their home and seeing the items couldn't hurt.

The welcoming couple showed me the beautiful home, well maintained in a stable part of Dallas. They had an added family room in the far back of the property and needed to downsize. They pointed out the pool table, red velvet barber chair, functioning barber pole, and gold antique register like in the movies. The register had served as a memory bank for their family, and they weren't sure what all it contained since it couldn't be opened, having been broken decades prior.

"The red velvet barber chair was inspired by the chairs at the Spaghetti Warehouse in Downtown Dallas," the husband reminisced.

"Mother and I upholstered it," smiled Myrtle. I realized I could use the chair and pole inside the shop, and we agreed on the price and a date for pick-up.

I recruited some friends to help me with the pick-up a few weeks later. One of them, a handy firefighter, was able to get their Gold Register open. They approached the register, unsure of what memories had just been unlocked. The look on their faces as they saw the different movie tickets, playbills, and coins was heart-warming. The memories they had shared with their daughters all came flooding back.

I kept the chair and barber pole in my loft as beacons of hope that I was one step closer. That pole would need a wall to be hung on, that chair needed impermeable reupholstery, and a suite to be put to good use.

After the eight-week business course was done, a few poignant moments of hope stayed with me, propelling me to keep going. When going confidently in the direction of your dreams, you will be surprised at how the universe shows its support. We want to help others reach their dreams. Others wish to see us reach ours.

Reach is a verb. Encouragement is there if we are seeking it.

Al's picture on the wall was a deeply personal attachment to me pursuing my calling, and I believe the Universe does encourage your calling when you take action. The 8-week Starting a Business Course was validation and asked more questions I needed to solve unbeknownst to me. A good question will always yield an even better one.

The upholstered antique barber chair and pole were so specific to what I was on the verge of creating, and I could not have asked for it, but it was there materialized. In pursuing the clarity of my goal, it was clear a business plan was needed to help me refine the product, and I would need help.

Being creative in an interpersonal trade means that analytical tasks such as business plan writing are daunting, but I have to act while scared. I must seek help and guidance from others along the journey in the same way I had to ask for directions on the way to El Salvador on the road trip with my family.

Diamonds In The Rough

- When going confidently toward your dreams, you will be surprised at how the universe shows its support. We want to help others reach their dreams. Others wish to see us reach ours.
- Reach is a verb. Encouragement is there if we are seeking it.

Discovery Questions

- What are opportunities at your disposal that you have not interacted with that could shine a light on your path? (books, people, classes, in-person, virtual)
- When was the last time you did something towards the creation of your dream?
- Who is a Julia in your life, someone similar to you pursuing their calling?

Frontera

Papi decidió que estaba muy oscuro para cruzar la frontera y sería mejor esperar hasta la mañanita. Nos estacionamos a la orilla de un ferrocarril abandonado para no estorbar a nadie. Mami y Tío Nicho se la pasan haciendo chistes a Papi, mientras Mami termina la cena de tortillas.

Noe se quedó bien dormido después de acabarse su biberón y Pablo y yo nos entreteníamos contándonos historias de terror, que si la llorona, que si el cucuy, que sí... "¡Niña! Te va dar mal de orin!!" me gritó Mami, pues estábamos sentados en el capó del Montero. "Mejor vayan a dormir para que llegue más rápido la mañana".

Al llegar a la frontera nos hicimos amigos de unos hombres que llevaban carros hasta jalando otros para revender. Llevaban dos carros llenos hasta el tope de encomiendas.

"Maestro, ¿hasta dónde van?"

"Amigo, vamos hasta Guatemala. Si es la primera vez que hacen el viaje prepárense para las mordidas, es más, de

Border

Papi decided that it was too dark to cross the border and that it would be best to await the break of dawn. We parked beside abandoned railroad tracks in order not to disturb anyone. Mami and Tio Nicho passed their time joking with Papi while we finished our tortilla dinner.

Baby Noe fell into deep sleep after finishing his bottle, and Pablo and I scared each other with what if La Llorona, or what if the cu cuy can track us, or what if... "Niña!!! You will get a bladder infection!!" yelled Mami since we sat on the hot hood of the Montero. "Best for y'all to go to sleep so that tomorrow arrives sooner."

As we arrived at the Mexican border we befriended a few men that were caravanning a few vehicles to Guatemala for resell. The cars were full to the brim of parcels from the States.

"Maestro, how far are y'all going?"

"Amigo, we are headed all the way to Guatemala. If it's your first time heading on this journey, prepare yourself for

una vez póngale unos pesos en los pasaportes cuando los paren para no batallar y que tengan buen viaje."

"Esa no me la sabía hermano, gracias por el consejo. ¿No le molesta si los seguimos?"

"Claro que no hermano, es más, deje y le enseñó en el mapa donde es mejor sacar la vuelta a un pueblito donde pueden salir en la autopista y aunque cobran un poco, las calles están muy lindas. Ya verá que llegaremos bien."

"Que Dios me lo bendiga maestro."

"Buen viaje y nos vamos viendo hermano."

the bribes, better yet, go ahead and place your cash in the passports when they stop you so they don't bother and have a great trip.

"I didn't know that trick hermano, but I thank you for the counsel. It doesn't bother you if we follow you here and there along the road?"

"Of course not hermano, better yet let me show you a route where you can get on a nice highway that charges some but the roads are pleasant. You'll see that we will arrive all good."

"May God bless you hermano."

"Good journey and we'll be seeing each other."

5.

EMBRACE WHEN SHIT GETS CONFUSINGLY CLEAR

"Yo sólo sé que no sé nada."
"All I know is I don't know anything."
-Pablo Benitez (Papi)

Knowing when to ask for help is as valuable as the help. As a child guiding my family toward a nation three countries away, I had to ask for help in various instances to navigate the map and translate that into progress. My father also partnered with Guatemalans caravanning a few vehicles to Guatemala to watch for each other and pace their progress.

"Gracias Maestro!" was his humble response to any insight or feedback he was given. He may not always apply it but he was always grateful.

"All I know is I don't know anything," was a common phrase Papi would repeat to us. Asking for help was a skill he demonstrated to us, and he would explain why. In those moments, I could not have known how this ability would help me in my personal journey.

After dreaming the recurring dream and visualizing it as detailed as the debilitating heat of Deep Ellum street tar on a mid-summer day, I mustered the courage to call someone else to help me with my plan.

Randy Moon was his name. I wouldn't be taken advantage of again and I let him know as much. Life can give you signs as obvious as a highway exit sign, but just like on a road trip, they can run up on you while you're in the center lane. If you miss it, you'll have to exit on the next one, make a U-turn, and come back around. However, missing that exit can be brutal anxiety in rush hour traffic on your way to work. My interaction with Moon was very similar.

Things do not "just" happen. You have to physically be in the car, literally on the road, on the way somewhere, for you to miss the exit. You can't miss the exit by looking up how to get there and not beginning. You don't arrive at the destination without heading that way. After a few trips around the block, you may decide that a ride to Telluride looks fun because you think it is a beautiful destination. You have to be headed in the direction of your dreams for the universe to conspire to assist you.

Here is what I mean.

I gave Randy a call and was pretty straightforward, firm, and strict with him in that I had already lost money to a scam artist business consultant. When I spoke to Randy, I explained to him that I wanted more or less someone to be my tutor.

"What do you mean?" he asked in a patient and active listening manner.

"I mean, I need to know where my business plan is coming from… maybe assignments where I gather my own information… I do need help with projections because I never feel comfortable with imaginary numbers," I explained.

We agreed to meet prior to my work shift on a Tuesday at a coffee shop off Knox Henderson, a swanky, high-end area.

"Thank you for adding color to our Vanilla sky…," mentioned a regular, "you are welcome any time!" He waved in the direction of all the other patrons as I waited in line at the coffeehouse. We laughed as we looked around and agreed I was the only nonwhite person in sight.

I was settling in by a window with an iced latte to help with the heat, to wait for Moon, the business consultant, to come and help me turn my vision into reality, when my phone rang. It was the owner of the paleteria, the one down the street from the Joyeria. I'd worked there in my childhood through my early twenties, selling wholesale jewelry to stay-at-home wives in an Avon-esque way, except the jewelry store was the distributor.

Get this. She and her partner owned a barber school next door. They were busy but couldn't get along and asked if I was interested in buying it. They were selling it. They were closing the doors tomorrow.

A well-dressed silver-haired gentleman walked into the coffeehouse while I was processing the call. We made eye contact and nodded. Randy Moon. As he sat down, I repeated what the caller was saying.

"So you are closing a barber school and looking for a buyer because the partners can't get along? How long has it had the same ownership?" Randy caught up with the conversation and started writing questions on a notepad for me to ask.

How much profit a month? How many students? What was overhead? Can we see it this evening?

We agreed to tour it that evening once I got off work.

Once off the phone, Randy and I had our formal introductions, got him a beverage, and he eagerly began to listen to my "why" all the way to my "what" for Blade Craft. He asked detailed questions to better understand my lack of budget, how he could help, and what I was trying to create.

Luxury barbering is my calling in that I can provide a haven of peace for those I serve, a respite from the toil of the mundane. Randy listened and took notes eagerly as I explained the lathers, tonics, and products tailored for men. Barbershops and men's lifestyle clubs abounded, but the training to care for the guests properly was not.

This was why it had to be an academy. This is why it had to be my vision made tangible. I explained what men were able and willing to pay for these services and how Cosmetologists had not been exposed to straight razor shaving or beard shaping.

He ran his fingers through his steel silvery locks," I could use a haircut!"

"Great! Let's go in before my shift, and I'll do it myself," I beamed and couldn't believe after I had just explained how and what we did that it was exactly what he wanted!

Upon arriving, I gave him a full tour and introduced him to the endearing Nicole and all the ladies working that day, all young, sweet, and attentive. My books didn't have an opening for close to a year, so arriving early was the only way. Throughout the service, I made sure to follow the establishment's service protocols and products. The plethora of aromatic hot towels, fresh lather, and scalp massage were all picture-perfect.

Men over fifty who can still boast of a full head of hair are lucky in that it does not matter what color it is, just that it's there. The silver finish brought out a handsome he forgot he had, and walking out, he purchased all the products to recreate the service at home.

"I'll meet you at the coffee shop at 7 right when you get out," he waved excitedly on his way out the door and thanked Ana, our outgoing front desk girl, for helping him with his purchase.

Now ready to start my day and review my books, I couldn't help but wonder why.

Why did I receive a call for a barber school on sale on this day?

Why, on the day I was meeting my consultant to write my business plan?

Why was the universe confusing me like this?

Should I buy it?

The lives of my guests were intertwined with our visits, and their goals, wishes, and hopes became my own. I genuinely believe that how they looked and felt after their service directly impacted their performance in their day-to-day. Life was a stage, and I was behind their curtain.

The end of my shift had arrived. Randy jumps into my car from the coffee shop lot, his hair still perfect. My day was successful in barbering, but my thoughts are plates that aren't landing neatly where I'd like them. Randy is thrilled playing out different scenarios. He was a natural tutor, and I am a natural student in that one of my top 5 strengths is learning.

We pull into the street parking in Oak Cliff down the street from the now out-of-business Joyeria. The ever-familiar street of my childhood was buzzing. The original Fiesta marketplace parking lot was full. The paleteria of my memories was there in full sight.

Consuelo greeted us in her conservative long skirt and natural colors. Her curls pinned back delicately as kitchen workers often do. I always wondered if her graceful leanness came from her business or the other way around.

"Pasa pasa!"

Introductions happened before the detailed grand tour. The drawers of the barber student stations were filled with hair, the basins showed years of wear, and the linoleum was lifting in various corners.

"We make $10,000 in profit a month, but my partner and I cannot agree," she explained, defeated.

Randy had more details to obtain. I was content. As we left, I knew.

I couldn't help myself.

I wanted to be sold.

I wanted to want it.

I wanted it to be handed to me.

That school was not meant to be mine, and I knew it. I'd maintain an open mind to see if I could be persuaded, but the visit further clarified my vision.

The sun had set, and it was night on Jefferson. The cars drove past a little too fast, and people walked a little too hurriedly. The street lights flickered on.

On the drive home, Randy was ecstatic thinking about how much we could save on overhead and start-up expenses. He explained how much the initial cost would sometimes kill a business, and we had something we could clean up and perfect.

"Randi, wasn't Nicole a total gem?" I asked.

He smiled, remembering, "Oh yes! She was so kind!"

"And wasn't Anna super sweet despite being slightly introverted?" I hinted.

"Anna was adorable! Helpful and attentive!" He declared.

"Now, Randy, can you see Anna or Nicole enjoying their walk to the car and their time in that building?"

His face and smile fell. "No. Absolutely not."

I knew at that moment that he understood. It had come full circle in one day for him. He got me.

"We have a lot of work to do, but I know we can do it," he assured.

Randy and my process was a unique one in that I needed to know and understand the plan and didn't just want it done for me. He guided and tutored me in gathering the information myself. He would then use his experience to polish it up and smooth it over.

During this season, I worked full time and would sit at Buzzbrews until I realized it was too late, even for a 24-hour diner, if they were now mopping.

I have kept a journal since I was a girl. It has helped me express my thoughts and study them before I myself am even aware of what they mean. It has served as protection to my heart and others from the words that could be unformulated thoughts not always exactly kind or welcome.

Jotting WOW (words of wisdom) is a practice I remain committed to. Bible verses, notes with friends, and anecdotes from clients eventually evolved into a major asset (my personal encyclopedia) in developing my business. More important to me than the creation of a "business" was the curating of a culture, a feeling, a lifestyle.

It also assisted immensely in keeping tabs on the various branches of business development, and it's a tool I use to this day.

There is nothing like going back to the journal three years prior to the same time I'm currently living to substantiate how smart, able, and dedicated I actually have been.

On our road trip to El Salvador, the map was paper, but we used it as a guide to arrive at our destination. In creating Blade Craft Barber Academy, the business plan was on paper as well, but it became the tangible checkpoint in creating something that wasn't there.   Thankfully the universe answered my asks with mentors to talk my ideas through and hold myself accountable.

Diamonds In The Rough

- Know when to ask for help.
- Keep track of your journey.

Discovery Questions

- The dream that you are after, is it clear? Are there different versions of it?
- Is there a map of sorts that you could be working on to head in the direction of your dream?
- How do you assess progress?
- How do you know you have arrived?

Cemento y Mordidas

El paisaje iba cambiando y el viento de mar iba espesando. Un talco soplaba y cubría todo. Hasta los árboles se veían indecisos en crecer.

Había fábricas de cemento por todos lados y nos preguntamos cómo la gente podía vivir aquí, pues el solo pensar en todo el trabajo que debía suponer tener que limpiar un hogar con todo ese polvo de cemento cada día parecía un fastidio y ni se diga el poder respirar bien.

Después de dar suficientes mordidas en el viaje hasta México, empezamos a preocuparnos que llegaríamos a El Salvador sin un cinco.

"Mi mamá va a estar contenta de ver lo grande que están los cipotes y al niño que aún ni lo conoce. En lo adelante debemos ir con más cuidado porque si no nos van a dejar sin nada y después para el regreso, ¡ja! Ahí si vamos a tener un problema."

Papá considerando la verdad de lo que mami acababa de decir, se empezó a preocupar un poco.

Cement and Bribes

The scenery was changing, and the breeze thickened from the ocean. A talc that blew threw covered everything. Even the trees seemed hesitant to grow.

There were cement factories everywhere and we asked ourselves how could people live here, because just thinking about the amount of work that it would take daily to keep a home clean must be fastidious and let's not even consider the difficulty breathing.

After continuing to tip the officers stopping us on our trip inside Mexico, we started to worry that we would arrive to El Salvador penniless.

"My mother will be really happy to see how much the children have grown, and she hasn't even met the baby. Ahead let's approach with more discretion because if not they'll leave us without a dime, and hmmm the problem will be the return."

Papi, considering the truth of Mami's words, started to worry a bit.

6.

MOVE THROUGH THE UNKNOWN

*"In learning you will teach,
and in teaching you will learn."*
– Phil Collins

Throughout my teenage years I got to work at a wholesale jewelry store located in the Latin American portal of Dallas. Walls of gold necklaces of varied lengths and styles, along with aisles of gold earrings, diamonds, watches, rings, and bangles, were our cubicles. My job consisted of weighing, measuring, labeling, and displaying the items. However, my favorite part of the job was assisting the customers, women like Mami, who sold the jewelry out of their homes like Mary Kay but for accessories. Entrepreneurship education was being given by me, as a 15-year-old to these women to help them keep track of their clients, payments, and items just as I assisted Mami at home.

The job had many perks, including the neighborhood providing an array of Latin American cuisine to choose from. All of the dishes nearby were made by someone's mother or grandmother, and they were seasoned with TLC.

One of the restaurants was the paleteria, and they served healthy food options. The owner was Consuelo, the barber school owner who called. I've always been aware of a vibration of connection throughout my life, and the paleteria was a delicious circle revisiting me in my adult life.

Naturally, years later, once a Barber Instructor myself, I stopped in to say hello, re-introduce myself, and leave my card, thus leaving the breadcrumb to follow. The freshness of the limon paleta was as sweet as ever. Buzzing with energy, the barber school on a Saturday had beautiful characters. I left having found more friends than I began with!

Being the first of my kind in the market meant that I would have to create the plan just as these ladies relied on asking for directions to make things clearer. The standard that existed for education in our business wasn't acceptable to me, nor was it close to what was possible.

As I continued to clarify my business plan, I found that doing something was way better than nothing. While I searched and waited for the funding solution to materialize, I worked on sourcing the best items for the student toolkits. The most elusive item was the old-school white barber smock. They had been discontinued in the US, and not even dentist smocks that were similar were available. Not only does a clean white smock look pristine, but it offers an immediate way to check the precision of the haircut or beard shaping. It provides a real-time checkpoint for balance or lack thereof while creating. I had always wanted one and was set on making it part of the uniform. The itchy shapeless loud fabrics of the smocks available simply wouldn't do. After researching, visiting, calling, and emailing contacts in Europe, it was clear that I needed a proper Tailor.

Tailors have many qualities that compare to a barber in that their trade requires in-person interaction and personalized services. The most obscure skill in both trades seemed to be reliability.

Inna was a Russian tailor who was able to create enough men's and women's smocks for close barber friends of mine to be part of a photo shoot in the case I ever opened. I had acquired antique pictures similar to the shapes I imagined would fit the mark, having never experienced them. She created clean, beautiful feminine and masculine forms. Just as she completed the project, she disappeared, and so began my tumultuous love affair with tailors.

One tailor could create the most unique and beautiful jobs but then couldn't turn them in on time. He also connived with other tailors in the town to not help me so that he could keep the business once fired, but still would not turn them in on time.

Another couldn't make them fit the people he measured. The next tailor had us go to her studio and constantly handhold to ensure that we received the projects. She was more interested in companionship than payment, and we couldn't afford the time.

Being the first in the market for detailed barbering education meant that I needed to inventory from my own experience the details that were missing and outline how to bring them to fruition. I felt like I was on a marathon blindfolded. Was I headed in the right direction? Had I even begun?

The women of the Joyeria reinforced a value my parents instilled in me through their journey and expeience of young immigrants navigating the unknown. Taking action in researching the smock creation for my future student's toolkits was a helpful form of project management, being both relevant and harmless enough.

Knowing that there is help at your disposal through the form of mentors will be the welcome salve to the pain of uncertainty. There was a sense of respect and honoring those before you by asking them for advice and guidance.

Diamonds In The Rough
- The experiences that you have spent the most time in will give you resources from which to draw on your journey.
- Personal interaction and experience with potential vendors and business relationships on a small scale will yield helpful information to make larger-scale decisions.

Discovery Questions
- What are some activities that you could be working on?
- Are there items on your business plan or outline that you could be assessing?
- Are there partnerships or connections you had prior that could be a smart idea to call on?
- Can you create a 5-step action plan to follow to act in intention in testing your service or product? Document the results, and start with the path of least resistance in order to test it.

El Miedo

En el siguiente paro decidimos no ofrecerles lana ni ponerlo en el pasaporte. Los militares caminaron alrededor de la troca. Habíamos llegado a un lugar remoto con árboles secos y una choza de palmas seca que les hacía de estación. Vestían uniformes, pero las metralletas decían más. En la misma parada nos encontramos a nuestros amigos guatemaltecos, los tenían detenidos con los baúles y las maletas abiertas. Era obvio que los guerrilleros estaban de humor, pues les habían destapado hasta los cobertores de gas.

"Buenas amigo."

"Buenas hermano."

Después de intercambiar unas palabras entre ellos, un guerrillero nos ordenó que apagáramos la troca y nos dijo que iban a inspeccionar nuestras cosas. Nos bajamos todos del auto y otros soldados se dirigieron a inspeccionar las maletas. El encargado separó a papá para hablar con él y vi como lo dirigía hacía un caminito, así que los seguí.

The Fear

On the next stop we decided that we would forego the cash in the passport routine. The soldiers walked around the montero. We had arrived at a remote place with dry trees and a palm shed as their patrol booth. They dressed in uniform but their ak's said more. In the same stop we found our fellow Guatemalan friends with their hoods and suitcases splayed open. We could tell the police were in a mood because they had even opened the gas tank covers.

"Good day my friend.'"

"Good day my brother"

After exchanging a few words with each other, the military police asked us to turn off the engine of the car and that they would be inspecting our belongings. We got out of the car and more soldiers directed themselves to examine our belongings. The guy in charge separated Papi to speak with him and I saw how he was directing him down a path so I followed him.

Fear is visceral and unmistakable. I recalled the torturous nightmares in which I would

El miedo es algo visceral e inconfundible. Recordé las torturantes pesadillas en donde amanecía sin él y el miedo pudo más que la obediencia o el respeto. El soldado me vio y se molestó que estuviera allí y en su acento Mexicano le ordenó a papi que me mandara con mi madre. Papi me tomó de la mano y me pidió que esperara con mamá. El soldado me dio la espalda y sin apartarle la vista empecé a caminar, pero a mitad del camino me escondí detrás de un árbol en donde se encontraba Pablito. El soldado se colocó en una posición en la que no le podíamos ver la cara a Papá. Escuché como le decían algunos insultos y después de un rato lo dejaron ir, creo que consideraron que era mejor enfocar su atención en los guatemaltecos.

Al volver a tomar la carretera nos dimos cuenta de la suerte que tuvimos.

"Alabado sea Dios," decía Mami. Tío Nicho se mantenía mirando el cielo azul al otro lado de la ventana, pero no decía nada.

awaken without him and the fear weighed more than obedience or respect. The soldier noticed me and ordered Papi to send me to Mami. The soldier gave me his back as I headed back towards Mami without losing him from view, but mid way I hid by a tree in which Pablo was also hiding alert. The soldier stood in a way that we couldn't see our Father's face. We heard yelling and insults and after a while they let him walk back, and they may have thought to focus their attention on the Guatemalans.

As we got back on the open road we realized just how much luck we'd had.

"Blessed be God," Mami said. Tio Nicho remained looking at the blue sky on the other side of the window but he never said a word.

7.

SEARCH FOR MENTORS

"There isn't anything more dumb than paying an attorney, then not doing what they advise."
-A Regular

The idea of mentors or guides was instilled in me from an early age, experiencing Mami's friends who were consistently 20-30 years her senior. They had the time and desire to show her the most kindness upon arriving in this country, so it isn't a surprise that I would feel the same. Market research is a search for projections, & invisible outcomes. The process requires inquisition and vulnerability when fact-finding with potential vendors. Still, it has beauty in that the purveyors of that information are people. People means connection.

My damn piece-mealed business plan was an agonizing process for me. Doug at the coffee shop would offer to help read it while I enjoyed a delicious cup.

In Farmers Branch, TX, there is a hole-in-the-wall cigar factory that rolls every single one by hand. Without the traditional added pesticides of huge manufacturers, House of Cigars creates a delicious smoke and does so in a personalized manner. The mad scientist behind the operation was Willie, but his wife Nicole (the real boss) and I became dear friends. I'd sit and smoke and write.

She'd greet guests and proofread my plans or ring them up while she answered questions. Nicole would refer to me only those souls who had passed her radar. She shared real-life experiences with me in ways that enriched my young, naive brain and protected my heart many times.

While continuing to find obstacles and seeking guidance on the path to create something that wasn't there, the universe presented me with guides in my everyday life.

I called on my dear friend Wes, who had generously explained design and branding just enough when we worked together to know when I was in over my head. I knew that I needed him to help me look "real."

I won't begin to try to explain what all goes into graphic design or brand identity in that I hardly understand it myself. Still, I can say that others "feel" what your brand represents when it is done well through images and color.

Legal counsel resulted from a friendship with a Regular who started and ran his own law firm. Mr. Law had me promise that I wouldn't agree to or sign anything with a potential partner until I'd let him review it.

Being afraid of legal fees, the complexities of the law, and not wanting to waste anyone's time, I waited until I completed the business plan. Then, he helped me incorporate and start the company with the state.

Yet another friend referred me to the accountant who had the patience to let me pick her brain throughout the process. I knew I wanted to be legit from the beginning and that I wanted to hit the ground running once I got the green light for funding. Barbara would let me bring us lattes to study the plan and start-up expenses. Even though the storefront was not ready, she explained that my current costs, like materials, filming, and legal, needed to be accounted for to ensure a smooth tax foundation.

After many edits and reprints later, Randy and I agreed that the plan was complete. It was even vetted through the attorney and accountant.

Who would I present it to?

Would I ever be able to figure it out?

What avenues would I seek for revenue?

I was proud and excited to test out my business plan, and I was actively seeking any and all forms of financing to get the ball rolling. I was also considering obtaining a partner. They might have experience in the areas I didn't to ensure I could provide the best education possible for the students while pampering our guests and caring for our future team.

Mr. Law was always kind during his visits, and haircuts became moments where we could discuss the current political climate, world events, polarizing documentaries, family, or business. Somehow, the conversation always arrived at discussing potential partners. And what a ride we were on!

The first potential partner arrived as a referral from a Hairdresser friend. After seeking guidance from Mr. Law on what to ask and discuss, I agreed to meet with Jim. He owned several small businesses and rental properties and raised his family in the DFW area. He was polite, business savvy, and appeared genuinely interested in the artistry of our industry. He seemed very keen on making this a partnership opportunity.

The next time I saw Mr. Law, he reminded me that a good deal today would be good tomorrow and that I didn't need to rush negotiations. After giving me more data to discuss, I agreed to meet with Jim again.

He brought a potential partnership agreement, and I could see his strengths were in the abstract projections and Excel spreadsheets. After the meeting, he suggested we meet with his wife the next time. She had always witnessed his business transactions, and I respected that he'd like to include her. Jim would be following up with details and an initial company agreement.

The email I received sounded a lot like I would be starting my dream Academy, only to try to avoid innumerable potential pitfalls to prevent him from taking it from me or for me to earn it back. While he offered to provide the funding, he expected me to handle all of the work but with highly complex targets that would barely cover my expenses.

Lunch with the wife arrived, and somehow, we were discussing the joys of taking dance lessons and how the man leads and the woman follows.

"Something tells me that you aren't a very easy dance partner to lead," Jim mentioned.

"It depends on the lead. I have been dropped flat on my back while dancing Bachata when I allowed myself to give up control to my dance partner," I clarified.

The rest of the meal, or how we parted ways, eludes my mind. It was clear that we weren't suitable for each other.

Mr. Law agreed.

Our next potential candidate arrived from the cigar lounge I frequented and loved the idea, the branding, and me. George was in Land Development and understood business on a macro level. We would meet for cigars to discuss my plan and the alternate details of it. Of course, we would also discuss his life and his current Commercial Developments. However, Mr. Law started picking up, a lot sooner than I did, that what we discussed or agreed to somehow got convoluted in the follow-up email exchanges.

We danced on the concepts and ideas for about seven months until Mr. Law stated that it would give him no greater pleasure than to send him a legal "fuck off" letter. George was wasting my time. After speaking to a mutual connection, they informed me that I had been beyond patient and that Mr. Law was right.

So the "fuck off" was sent.

While continually gathering prices and information to ensure accuracy, I had yet to determine when I'd be able to actually purchase a thing. I called the international textbook manufacturer I admired most for their legacy and completeness.

Heather was the sales representative, and I made sure to have her call me back when she was bored because I wasn't anybody who could buy anything yet. Still, I was working on a Business Plan to make my dream academy a reality. Graciousness and kindness don't begin to describe her patience with me in reviewing the materials and prices. She even arranged to have samples sent to my home.

We began a friendship where she would check on me when there were sales, she in the cold New York, and I, of course, in the depths of Texas. I got to share my self-made website with her, which had great photography with entry-level coding, but it was a start.

Jim at ALA Beauty in Plano, TX, was and still is a tremendous resource for me. He has been in the equipment and appliance industry for decades. He has always been very generous with his experience and knowledge. He quoted me for start-up prices for my academy and even promised to match them no matter how long it took me to reach my goal. How was I so lucky to find such an incredible guide!? The warehouse, a barber's playground, was full of antique barber chairs, stations, and relics from times past, as well as the latest and greatest.

Continual work has always been a solace for me and a source of accomplishment. I got to enjoy working on my craft through clients and services. On my days off, I developed a detailed curriculum for the Academy while pretending it would be immediately useful.

Altruist was a Regular who worked endless hours, days, and decades. From the moment he came in, I understood he just needed calm, quiet, and peace.

So much beauty comes from asking oneself, "What does my client need?" and being able to provide it. Being a woman in a man's world has given me backstage access and insight into understanding dynamics that aren't black and white. What does a young woman have in common with a man or even a young boy?

Al, as he asked me to call him, had good weeks where we'd discuss art, favorite family trips, and, eventually, my obsession with Blade Craft. We'd talk business and the enjoyment of working with our hands. We laughed at the joys of being useful. Our parents were ongoing comedies, and our siblings were characters needing ever-present follow-up.

"A space is just a box, Lilly, so don't fall in love with it. YOU are the pudding. YOU are the product."

We'd talk politics, traffic, and news. We got teary-eyed over aging pets and understood all too well the need to baby our shih tzus. But, sometimes, he'd just need calm. Sometimes, after a whole service in silence, I'd finish styling his hair and say, "NOW... I think that you are HERE. Welcome home."

Eventually, as the years wore on, he preferred that I even check him out if it meant he didn't have to speak to anyone else. On some visits, I was a fly on the wall, with his phone on speaker, to company negotiations and trade talks. We wouldn't exchange a single word while the service was executed in silence to not let the other side know he was getting his hair cut.

Things had gotten beyond intense at work, and he just wanted calm. No matter the holidays or the overwhelming seasons, he'd always thank me for the slice of peace during the service. He reminded me there would be nothing like the satisfaction of building something myself.

It became like a mantra. Seeing him when I needed the encouragement most would be one of life's merciful gifts, for it was he on the wall outside of the Starting a Business Course at SMU. He was so proud that I had pushed past my discomfort and encouraged me.

"What is the worst thing that can happen, Lilly?"

"I can lose everything."

"How much you got?"

"I ain't got shit!"

"Exactly!"

A piecemeal plan started taking shape with close connections sharing some of their skills with me through the process. Continual progress in completing my business plan allowed me access to establishing an incredible foundation for the academy. My dream was becoming a reality. But, I would have to get creative in raising the funds because it could be dangerous to put all my trust in a single source.

Diamonds In The Rough

- Guides materialized for me in the form of older, more experienced entrepreneurs willing to look at my business plan as well as those who do what I needed for a living because they sympathized with what I was trying to create.
- Just because someone checks the boxes of what you think might be a strategic partner does not mean they are. You can always say no.

Discovery Questions

- Is there anyone in your life whose lifestyle you admire?
- What about that person gives you the perception that they are ahead or more expertly situated than you are?
- What would you expect or desire from it if you could meet with them for a 30-minute phone call monthly?
- Do you have expectations from a mentor? Personal expectations for yourself as a result of having a mentor?
- On branding, do you understand what a style guide from a design firm is?

Desvio

El deseo de llegar se interrumpió con el sueño y el hambre. Nos paramos en un hotelito de carretera y buscamos en el libro telefónico la comida favorita de Mami, pollo frito. Encontramos un lugar donde nos lo traerán directamente a la puerta. Mientras esperábamos, tomamos turnos para irnos bañando y la ansiedad por cenar crecía con cada minuto que pasaba. Esperamos por más de dos horas, hasta que finalmente llegó un muchacho en bici con la comida, nos la entregó y rapidito siguió su camino. Al empezar a comer nos fijamos que los pedacitos de arroz en el pollo no eran arroz, si no gusanitos, con la misma hambre que nosotros. El cansancio venció el asco y nos tuvimos que conformar con tortillas. No todo lo que anhelamos en verdad lo es.

A la mañana siguiente buscamos un puestecito para desayunar donde hacían las tortillitas frescas al pedirlas. Nos perdonamos el error de la noche anterior y partimos nuevamente rumbo a El Salvador. Como hacía falta la comida de Mami.

Detour

The desire to arrive was interrupted by sleep and hunger. We stopped at a small street motel and found Mami's favorite food, roasted chicken, in the phone book. We found a place that delivered the food to our door. While we waited, we took turns in the shower, and the anxiety to eat grew with each passing minute. We waited over two hours until, finally, a guy on a bicycle arrived, handed us the food, and was quickly back on his way. Once we had begun eating, we realized that the rice grains were full of maggots with the same hunger as ours. Fatigue outweighed our disgust, and we consoled ourselves to be happy with eating plain tortillas. Not everything we desire is actually what we desire.

The next morning, we found a street vendor for breakfast that created handmade tortillas as you ordered them fresh. We forgave ourselves for our mistake from last night and headed back on the road to El Salvador. We really missed Mami's cooking.

8.

GET CREATIVE

"Antes muerta que sencilla."
"Better dead than basic."
-all of the confident women in the world

The fundraising plan was solidified and waiting to be executed. I used all I'd learned at The Starting a Business Course at SMU to put it together. Interestingly, during this season of inception, I thrived in busy, anonymous settings. There was enough activity to keep my mind going, yet not enough interruptions to distract me.

During another long night with my thoughts on the future and my eyes on the screen at Buzzbrews, my favorite diner, a patron had drawn my profile on a sheet of paper and gifted it to me once completed. How long had I sat so still that he could capture my expression without my awareness? It was then, yet again, that I knew it was time to head in for the night. I took the gift with a smile and soon hurried away. This encounter felt like one of those moments in scary movies where the protagonist ignores the signs warning her of something awful.

When brainstorming on maximizing a crowdsourcing opportunity, I needed to think outside of the box for ways to engage those unfamiliar with barbering.

How could I introduce the public to the beauty and intricacies of this centuries-old trade?

In the fall of 2012, crowdsourcing websites made coming up with start-up capital easy for many innovative ideas. There was an item I followed that looked like a glorified wrist sweatband used for a wallet. I witnessed its ascent to a product that was available for purchase. The process was an online platform where you could create different campaigns that offered various perks to persuade users to invest in your idea to have it come to fruition. The platform took a percentage of your sales, and once you discounted your cost, the campaign hopefully yielded a profit. There was this feeling of belonging to a group of creatives who were "doing" instead of "dreaming."

Considering myself tech-tarded, I definitely didn't have a camera or any equipment for capturing digital media content that was required to sell your idea when the droves of sponsors landed on my page. Crowdfunding had become a recent development, and videos were the way to share an idea, but I would give it my own twist. Being the kinesthetic person I am, I opted for hands-on interaction to amplify the campaign running online simultaneously. Lilly on Location would be an immersive experience that would demonstrate what Blade Craft Barber Academy would teach, driving potential sponsors to the site if they missed the in-person event.

After asking on FB if anyone could help create a video for a crowdsourcing site, a childhood friend, Marv, offered to film it. Clients who were like family volunteered to obtain their services while on cámara for my crazy goal.

I had the perfect outfit picked out all down to the nude studded Louboutins. My cousin sold shoes at a high-end store, and I had recruited his help in choosing them in hopes that he would talk me out of purchasing my exorbitant craving. He did the opposite.

We filmed the video in two parts in order to preserve my friends' time and the hospitality of Nicole and Willie at the House of Cigars.

I took pride in being employed at a luxury lifestyle barbershop while coordinating my informal education and fundraising efforts. It was crucial to me to perform at peak performance on the job and not have my dream project negatively impact my opportunity. Boss, the owner and creator of the brand, had always answered the phone when I called. He understood that I had committed to at least two years of dedicated application before leaving to pursue my own project.

My respect for him meant that I valued his time, and I didn't want him to interact with my idea until it was ready. Like a delicious cake, the presentation was of the utmost importance and could not be sloppy. Working at his company exposed me to facets of service I had never had access to and products that arrived from crazy corners of the world to offer the most intricate experience. I didn't want my exit to even begin to be on his radar until I had the fundraising packaged, the branding, and the plan solidified enough for me to speak confidently on the matter.

There was also the issue of survival. You see, he could fire me. I could lose touch with my prized clients and the solace of arriving at a beautiful shop and performing, all while dealing with the chaos of creation once away.

When I was a young girl, I often asked Papi where the women in the bible were. Mami and I felt strong and fierce in many ways, but all the cool stuff seemed to be done by boys.

One of the stories he read to me was the beautifully illustrated story of Esther in a Spanish children's bible stories book.

It's a story of the beautiful Jewish wife of a Persian king who must persuade the king to retract an order for the general annihilation of her people throughout the empire. My preparation before speaking to my boss reminded me of this process. No, it wasn't the preservation of a people, but instead, my surviving financially enough to get to the starting line of creating something that wasn't there before while preserving the relationship.

"Go, gather all the Jews to be found in Susa, hold a fast on my behalf, and do not eat or drink for three days, night or day. I and my young women will also fast as you do. Then I will go to the king, though it is against the law, and if I perish, I perish." - Esther 4:16 ESV.

For the second part of filming, we called three of my closest regulars and asked them to join us at the House of Cigars for services, camaraderie, and quality smokes. Noe arrived to carry and place the barber chair and supplies to stage them for filming. Marv came with his jovial spirit and guided them as to what he thought best. Willie, Nicole, and Viktoria, the Russian, helped and cheered us on.

"Mira mami! Laugh and smile like you always do with them at the shop!! The camera picks up that energy!" guided Willie from his decades in entertainment. We were smoking, laughing, shaving, and filming when we saw none other than Boss pull up in the parking lot.

"Mami! It's your boss!!! Oh shit!!!," Willie exclaimed, "He could fire you if he thinks you work here cutting hair!!!"

"It's ok. It's my day off, and he will eventually see the product," I gulped nervously.

Meanwhile, Boss paced on the phone in the parking lot and grabbed the door handle, but before walking in, he paced on the phone, stuck his head to wave inside, then walked back to his car, hopped in, and drove off.

"Huh? What the fuck just happened?" asked Nicole. Viktoria and I stared at each other and couldn't believe our luck.

"I'm unsure, but the show must go on," directed Marv.

No need to ask for forgiveness today.

The days coming up to the filming, I fractured my right foot on the very top after chasing my shih tzus around my loft. After icing it and wrapping it for days, my blackish-blue foot fit in the heels and hid well in the low-cut heel. Thankfully, sitting while filming managed to conceal my limping or bluing bruise. We finished the video.

Once starting on the path of creating a video for my fundraising concept, I was in for a surprise when my livelihood was threatened, yet I couldn't turn back.

Starting a business feels like feeling in the dark for the restroom at an Airbnb. You have the need, but you also might run into a door. The fundraising process was one of the means I explored for funding, and I was terrified of letting everyone in on it.

Diamonds In The Rough

- Research + People = Connection
- Hideouts can provide consistency.
- Fundraising ideas are as unique as your idea.

- Things don't always work out like you fear they might, but that can be great.

Discovery Questions

- What is your favorite bee hive or hideout setting where you have anonymity and can get your creative juices flowing?
- What is a creative way to get your product or service funded?
- What is your favorite underdog story, and what was the solution? (Think Esther for me)
- What activities could you guide your friends easily to assist you with?

Tacos

La comida de mami me ha resuelto varios asuntos durante mi vida. Para empezar están las lecciones de ventas que he ido aprendiendo desde los 4 años, que es cuando empecé a acompañarla a los "jonques" (junk yards) llenos de trabajadores hambrientos. Su salsita, hecha al día, acompañaba la delicia de sus tacos de jamón con huevo, "briskit", o los más famosos, carne con papa; que saciaban al cien por ciento acompañados de la frescura de una Dr. Pepper. Su dedicación porque todos los ingredientes fuesen frescos era inamovible. Apreciaba ver cómo su rostro se llenaba de orgullo cuando le decían lo delicioso que estaban.

"¿Pues quien lo hizo?" decía mientras se encogía de hombros.

"¿Y tu mami tiene novio?" me preguntó una vez un señor árabe dueño de un lugar nuevo.

"¡Sí! Mi papá." le contesté a lo obvio.

Imagínese una hielera llena de tacos recién hechos, y otra hielera llena de sodas con

Tacos

Mami's home cooking has resolved many problems throughout my life. For starters, there are the endless salesmanship classes I have been taking since at least four years of age when I accompanied her to junk yards full of hungry mechanics. She made daily salsa, accompanied by her delicious tacos of ham and egg, brisket, or her most famous beef and potato, which satisfied 100% with an ice-cold Dr. Pepper. Her dedication that all ingredients were of the utmost freshness was unwavering. I appreciated how her face lit up when people exclaimed how delicious they were.

"Well, who made them?" she shrugged.

"Does your mom have a boyfriend?" asked the Arab owner of one of the pick n' pulls.

"Of course! My Dad!" I responded to the obvious.

Picture this- an igloo cooler full of freshly made tacos and an additional one full of ice and sodas that Pablo manned. Our system was simple. Mami

hielo que Pablo se encargaba de mantener.

Nuestro sistema era sencillo. Mami manejaba, y yo me bajaba y corría adentro para dejarles saber lo que teníamos al día. Encargaban lo que gustaran, y yo corría de regreso al carro para dar la orden, y al regresar ellos me daban el dinero. Cuando empecé a escribir, aprendí a dejarles fiado para que me pagaran el Viernes. Mami se molesto mucho conmigo, pero quedo impresionada cuando me lo pegaron ya acordado.

Si alguna vez le pedíamos PB & J para llevar a las excursiones de la escuela, mami aclaraba que la comida de gringos no tiene nutrición y sabe feo. Así que nos mandaba con taquitos y una Dr. Pepper, cada uno envueltos en papel de aluminio para que mantuvieran su respectivo clima, obvio.

Nunca ordenamos pizza en nuestro hogar hasta que tuve edad suficiente para ordenarla yo misma. Tampoco teníamos tarjetas de crédito pues no gastamos más de lo que teníamos. Me resulta gracioso recordar que cuando rentamos películas Papi siempre se aseguraba de

would pull up to the auto salvage places, and I'd jump out, run inside, and give them the spill on what we had that day. They'd order what they wanted. I'd return to the car to pick up the order, and they'd give me cash on delivery. As I started learning to write, I kept tally marks if they didn't have cash so they could pay me on Friday.

Mom was pissed the first time, but when they paid up Friday, she was shocked.

If we ever requested a PB&J to take on school field trips, Mami clarified how gringo food didn't have the nutrition we needed and tasted awful. Instead, she would pack us tacos and a Dr. Pepper, each wrapped in aluminum foil to help each maintain its respective temperature, obviously.

We didn't receive a pizza in our home until I was old enough to call and place the order myself. Also, there were no credit cards in our home to make these transactions less complex or more normalized. The first time we went to Blockbuster was a treat for us, and my dad was religious about getting things back on time.

devolverlas a tiempo "para no quedar mal".

Teníamos hambre. Todo este polvo y el viaje y estar todos pegados ya deseaba sentarme en un sofá y estirarme a gusto.

Como nos hacían falta esos taquitos...

Soñando desde el asiento de atrás...

We were hungry. All this dust and driving and closeness made me long to sit on a couch and fully stretch.

We could use the tacos now...

Backseat daydreaming...

9.

IF YOU'RE GOING TO DO THIS, REALLY DO THIS

"Piensa antes de hablar."
"Think before you speak."
-Papi to me infinite times

After we completed the video and the swag supplies for the crowdsourcing event started arriving, I decided on the month I would drive all my efforts towards launching the Lilly on Location Fundraising campaign alongside the digital campaign. I could only hope to make a dent in building or obtaining a loan.

I had:

- Started saving
- Created a business plan
- Survived two business consultants

- Found a trustworthy accountant and patient attorney
- A beautiful branding package
- Website
- Business cards
- Curricula Creation per each program
- Service system outlines
- Decided that crowdsourcing was a more aggressive tactic for my goal
- Hypothetical locations for Lilly on Location events
- Considered potential partner candidates
- And somehow, I still had my basic necessities and the drive to do this

I was ready to share my concept with my boss. He agreed to meet me for coffee, and I prayed that being prepared would help.

Discipline & organization aren't qualities you can buy, and no one can help you develop them. You can't ever see time saved, but you can suffer the agony of time wasted. My preparations were not a waste of time.

I told him everything I wanted to create in the Academy, how all the graduates would be an asset to his concept, and about my crowdsourcing Lilly on Location idea. I also explained the classes I had taken and that I had a plan.

I mentioned that the co-worker I knew could shadow me in introducing my regulars to them since I could not take his clientele with me. We had both experienced firsthand how the lack of education and training plagued our industry. That straight razor shaving and haircuts were not just services, and barbers were not just service providers but so much more.

Through my time at the company, I learned that timing and how things are communicated can sometimes be even more important than what we say. I had not said a word to the team because I wanted his direction on if and when to mention it. Future ideas and change can bring confusion and worry to the current moment. Respect and gratitude were the two main qualities I wanted to instill in my conversation with him.

He was so kind and encouraging. He appreciated my coming to speak to him first. He made sure I understood his expectations and offered the location I had been working in as one of the stops for Lilly on Location.

We agreed on his timing to announce my departure and introduce my current regulars to the lucky team members who would align with each regular once that time came. Being a full-blooded entrepreneur, he knew there was always a space between said & done.

How lucky could I be? Not only had I not lost my job, but I had instead earned an ally. The story of Esther speaking to the King from my childhood stories also yielded me a visual of how to take caution when talking to my boss, who had provided me with an exceptional work opportunity. The respect and gratitude that I painstakingly prepared to express would be multiplied in my experience to follow.

Diamonds In The Rough

- Preparation and tactful communication succeeded in a better outcome than I could have dreamt of.

Discovery Questions

- Is there anyone you are hesitant to communicate about launching your project?

- Can you voice record yourself having the hypothetical conversation and listen to it back to brainstorm how to communicate effectively and compassionately?

Cerca de Guatemala Y Amigos Raros

Recorrimos millas y millas por las plantaciones de guineo y plátano e íbamos viendo cómo finalmente el paisaje se iba pareciendo más y más a El Salvador. Veíamos los pájaros con sus colores intensos y empezábamos a sentir con cada milla recorrida el tierno y anhelado cambio.

En cada parada docenas de niños iban corriendo a vendernos naranjas, las naranjas más sabrosas, dulces y frescas. Apreciamos la inocencia de estos niños, sucios, pobres, pero felices.

Durante tantas horas de camino llenábamos las cubetas de gasolina por si en algún momento nos encontrábamos lejos de alguna gasolinera. Obvio el asiento donde empezamos cada uno el viaje iba cambiando con cada parada, menos el de Papá. Pablo cabía encima de las maletas atrás y sé podía acostar y estirarse a jugar con sus juguetes y Mami a veces se venía al asiento de

Near Guatemala & Unlikely Friends

We traveled through miles and miles of plantain fields, and we could see how the terrain was changing in appearance the closer we got to the coast, which resembled El Salvador. We saw an array of birds with intensely colorful feathers, and we began to feel with each passing mile the wanted change.

At each speed bump, dozens of children would run to sell us the most savory, sweet, and fresh oranges. We appreciated the innocence of these children, dirty, impoverished, but happy.

During the many road trip hours, we would refill the empty gasoline tanks in case we were ever far from a gas station. Obviously, the seat we each began in would change with each stop, except Papi's. Pablo could even fit on top of all the luggage in the back of the montero, and it afforded him a bunk bed of sorts where he could lay down and stretch to play with his toys. Mami would sometimes join us in the back seat to rock the baby to

atrás para arrullar al niño o dormirse con él en brazos.

En ocasiones, bajábamos los vidrios para disfrutar del viento y para ahorrar gasolina. Mi tío nos contaba chistes o pasadas y podía reírme con el rostro contra el viento para después sentirlo dormido. En uno de esos momentos, tío ha decidido escupir por la ventana como suelen hacer los hombres y yo que iba detrás con el cristal abajo sentí como el escupitajo me cayó directamente en la cara. El asco y la risa suelen ser amigos raros.

sleep or to fall asleep with him in her arms.

Occasionally, we would lower all the windows to feel the air and use less gas. My uncle would tell us jokes or stories, and I could laugh with the wind against my face, only to feel it numb later. On one of the face-in-the-wind occasions, my uncle sitting in front of me decided to spit out of the window like men do, only for it to land square in my face. Disgust and laughter are unlikely friends, but friends nonetheless!

10.

REMEMBER: YOU'RE RUNNING A MARATHON BLINDFOLDED

"Don't allow your mind to tell your heart what to do.
The mind gives up easily."
-Paulo Coelho

I had the green light to communicate with my friends now on my idea and plan. One night before a show, a friend and I were getting ready, and I told her how the crowdfunding site would be live early that night to ensure function. The following Saturday was the first week of Lilly On Location, and I had no idea how it would fare.

Tera immediately logged on, was the first seed planted into my dream, and gave me a pep talk that thinking on draws tears to this day. Lilly on Location was live, and the universe did not disappoint.

Once the idea of Blade Craft Barber Academy was announced, I was floored by the support people offered me through that time. They shocked me. Charm shared his connection with a bespoke men's clothing line.

My friends invited DJs to ensure the events were successful, as well as their networks. One location even curated a unique cocktail to showcase the Blade Craft Mason jars that served as swag for supporters.

My childhood friends Mirella, Amy, Alma, and Eli all showed up during their weekends to operate the swag booth, schedule the guests wanting to receive services and lend me constant encouragement. These efforts meant everything to me because I had no clue how to create this dream alone.

At the House of Cigars, I performed 22 Straight Razor shaves. What I would do to have kept count of all the shaves I have performed in my lifetime! It was heartwarming to see my loyal regulars interact with my childhood friends. My brothers always helped set up and take down despite crazy times and locations, no matter how random, a constant heartbeat of life energy to flame my dream.

It should have been obvious.

No one had seen the facade as vividly as I envisioned it. No one experienced the academy in dreams as I did. It became clear that as much as I would invite people to the fundraising efforts, they always asked, "What time will YOU be there."

You see, if you are reading this and assuming that there is some THING or PLACE that matters more than who you are, you couldn't be more mistaken. People connect with YOU, the person. YOU, the little girl that sells tacos to mechanics, you the healer, you the artist, it is your voice and presence that wins.

The Alchemist by Paulo Coelho says that the universe will conspire to help you if you go after your soul's calling. It is true. Except the universe has shown up in my life as a human being, as an opportunity, and not some extraterrestrial out-of-body experience.

It has shown up as conversations with my most encouraging uncle, even though it was I who always had to pick up the phone and make the call.

The campaign was coming to a close, and I was looking forward to the last weekend to knock it out of the park.

Driving a 2009 Dodge Challenger on the Dallas North Tollway was a sense of freedom. Dressed to the nines for the day, having awoken with the recurring vision, it felt like it would be a good day. On my way to work, lost in thought, drivers encouraged my speed by moving out of the way.

My phone rang. It was Sally, the business banker contact for one of my regulars. The friendly voice on the other end made me at ease with the inevitable "no" I knew I would be receiving. But, as I approached my exit, she said something different.

"You are doing everything you are supposed to, Lilly. You are on the right track. I only loan in the million and above, but you are on your way." I don't remember ending the call. I don't remember using my right-turn blinker. I do remember the tears clouding my view and wiping them away, hopeful to have heard something different than a no.

"No" means not right now. Red lights suck.

Jefferson became a dear friend after multiple visits. He had also built his business from the ground up, and his obstacles and nemesis were out of a movie.

It became clear that he found my obsession with creating Blade Craft amusing, and he asked at least three times to review my business plan before I found it rude not to meet to review it with him. He was tall, funny, and no bullshit.

"Do not think you aren't worth a shit," he'd say.

"Stop and look around. Everything you see is owned by someone. It was created through the direction of a being. The average lifespan in America is 80 years. If you get to the end of your lifetime and didn't create or acquire something that makes you proud, you'd have only yourself to blame."

"It's all bullshit," about how things weren't what they seemed.

"They're chicken shits," meaning people don't take action but they want to bitch about it.

"Whatever business you think you're in, you're wrong. You have only one job to do every day. That job is to find more money."

Bingo. I had met someone else who felt that cash flow was pertinent. It felt great to discuss reality, as shitty as it sounds.

Lilly on Location events allowed an opportunity for connection and to create micro experiences of what was to come. But with all of the unknowns in creating something that wasn't there, sacrifices are bound to appear

Diamonds In The Rough

- Who you are is what attracts support, and affirmations will continue to guide you.
- Encouragement from the universe not only manifested as my community showing up to support my fundraising efforts, but I even received a phone call.
- I connected to someone who resonated with my desire to materialize my dream.
- Friends go above and beyond because they see how much I want this.

- The amazing souls that helped fuel my fire before it became visible will forever hold a place in my heart and memory.

Discovery Questions

- Is there an action you need to take to find revenue?
- What are two forms of affirmation you have received lately that confirm you are on the right path?

Tapachula Y Migrañas

Llegando a Tapachula sabíamos que ya estábamos cerca de Guatemala y que para él amanecer estaríamos llegando a la segunda aduana, ya nos faltaba menos de un día.

El mapa, que ya estaba todo arrugado y sucio, no nos había mentido y ya casi finalmente conocíamos Guatemala.

A pesar de que papi manejaba bastante bien, las migrañas me encontraban en todas partes del camino por más que las huía. Había padecido de convulsiones y por el dolor descubrí que por más que quisiera leer en el carro no me era posible. Así que no me quedaba más que mirar por las ventanas, contarnos chistes y cantar como locos todo lo que se nos ocurría.

Tapachula & Migraines

Arriving in Tapachula, we knew that we were getting closer to Guatemala and that by morning, we would arrive at the second border in less than a day.

The map was wrinkled and dirty; it had not lied to us, and we would finally be introduced to Guatemala.

Despite Papi being a great driver, the migraines could find me through many parts of the journey despite my attempts to hide from them. They had gotten as bad as causing convulsions, and because of the pain, I learned that it would be impossible for me to read in a moving car. That meant I could look out the window, engage in jokes, and join in singing to entertain ourselves.

11.

BE WHO YOU ARE

*"Everyone seems to have a clear idea
of how other people should lead their lives,
but none about his or her own."*
– Paulo Coelho

Well, shit ass. The fundraising campaign came and went. I ended up breaking even in that I raised what it cost me to launch it; however, now I also had all those that knew me asking for a timeline. Everyone seemed to believe that Blade Craft Barber Academy would launch any day now. If only…

I needed to keep searching for more options. Creating the academy wasn't just a dream that I dreamt. Nope, I just had to go and let everyone else know that I was truly committed to this invisible concept, and people only saw me.

Since I needed to validate my insanity, I continued my research.

"Why wouldn't you consider marriage a lucrative option for startup capital?" He was bemused. Dan was the volunteer business advisor the Small Business Development Center assigned to me, and it was a checkmark I needed to qualify for a small business loan if I ever decided to go that route.

Dan meant well, and as a native Texan, I was accustomed to taking these types of comments as a means of endearment. He was well into his seventies, retired, and the only things shiny about him were his college & wedding rings. The stuffy office made me so grateful to make a living as a barber.

"Don't laugh, Lilly, I'm serious. Consider it."

"Of course, I will, but do you have any ideas on what is actually required to obtain an SBA loan? What is the timing after I save the down payment?… Anything in the form of a timeline… moving target..?" I asked, attempting to get some insight instead of a matchmaker or nuptial advisor. After a well-meaning lecture, some paper shuffling, and book suggestions, I walked out with my dose of chauvinism for the day.

When embarking on a journey to create something that isn't there, the waiting is more painful than a no, yet it is by being your authentic self that the path reveals itself.

I get it. A heavily tattooed 20-something-year-old with half a shaved head isn't exactly the textbook definition of business casual. My failed visit with the patriarch left me with no more guidance on acquiring funding for my startup than before I visited.

I'd seen a few commercials online that Wells Fargo was the SBA preferred lender, and well, the commercials couldn't be wrong. I parted my hair opposite my shaved side to conceal that I may be a deviant, wore a long sleeve button down to hide my tattoos, and a pencil skirt that screamed ROI. After checking in at the bank, they informed me that the business banker was not in and they had zero guidance on any requirements on how to apply for an SBA loan… to check with another branch.

Three branches later, it was clear that while the SBA preferred them, they did not prefer the SBA because they had no clue what was required to obtain a business loan, or who could tell me. I was interested in an SBA loan because it was supposed to have a low-interest rate and was secured by the feds. While that sounds terrifying, it brought me solace in that if they approved my business idea, it was a validation that I wasn't totally crazy.

A bank is a place that lends you money when you do not need it. Time wasted was extremely obvious. I kept searching for other opportunities.

How many doors can be closed before one finally opens? I was at the Across the Street Diner in Corsicana working on detailing the curricula. I'd left town to get peace from the rejection of the universe.

Small-town Texas can be healing and soothing. I sat through their morning and lunch crowds, all the while working. Everyone knew each other. Little kids were made to greet the Judge when all they wanted was pie, but it was the South, after all, and the kindness of manners earns us our pie. Just like they arrived, they all went back on their ways. It was another welcome hideout that could renew my sense that things can be different.

Vibrations of energy varied through the groups of people arriving within two-hour periods, then calmed when they were gone. I have always wondered why everyone goes in and out of work at the same time, causing traffic on the streets and hold-ups in the coffee shops. Why wouldn't different trades all pick different hours?

I got the same buzz when I was in New York facing a window, worker bees busy on their way, yet the anonymity lets me focus on my work instead of my guilty pleasure - connection.

After the lunch rush, the waitress escorted me to a private area of the restaurant that was so quiet and empty that I realized I'd been there as long as her shift. I tipped and thanked her for letting her coworker know where I was and giving me the ability to ask for help if I needed anything. At last, the ebb and flow allowed me hours of uninterrupted progress on my curricula and outlines for my plan.

Once done, I walked into the antique store in front of my car, which caught my eye when I parked. It was full of history, stories, and options!

"Hello, sir. I'd like to see anything barber-related you may have," I asked the mutilated gentleman at the counter. He had survived some agonizing atrocity with burns to his face, making it very difficult to understand him and make eye contact.

He brought me antique curling irons and blow dryers, all with a kindness in his voice. I clarified I needed male-related items for a barber, which he conceded and went back to search past the rusted straight razors.

Before me were handheld clippers in stainless steel forged to last from before there was electricity. How many haircuts had they done, and how many hands had they been in? Had they belonged to one barber stingy with his tools, or had they been shared?

I held the tissue paper-wrapped items on my way to the car, excitedly thinking of ways they may be used or repurposed, and felt gratitude for the hope they represented for me. They, too, may take a different form than they currently have in a future reality.

Throughout my continued research, I learned that Austin seemed to be a hub for micro-lending, and I found a company willing to look at my plan. They had clear guidelines on what the SBA required for a startup loan, and I was thrilled. Finally, some parameters. Finally, some rules. Thankfully, the savings and startup capital I had raised helped my case.

I also learned that it is easier to borrow for something that doesn't exist yet than for something already established, which made no sense to me, but no one cared.

The loan officer I was paired with was stern but friendly, and I regained hope that I may actually achieve it. Mari was funny, too, and patient with my ignorance of the process.

Applying for a loan of that caliber felt like a continual assignment that requested more and more items from prior years, like tax returns and a report card from grade school (kidding), but honestly, it felt like they would then go back and request more.

Despite not wanting to marry for money to open my business, I obtained check marks without failing my true self while still progressing towards the goal.

Lilly on Location had been a successful event in bringing brand awareness, but I still had not secured the funding I was after. The project had paid what it cost to put on, yet not enough to jumpstart it. I had to put the next foot forward in pretending the information I was gathering was immediately necessary as though the funding was just at arm's reach.

In the waiting is where we discover what we can endure to experience the dream in the flesh.

Diamonds In The Rough

- I was able to obtain check marks towards understanding my business plan without failing my true self.
- I was willing to tone down some socially unwelcome stereotypical appearance traits such as my shaved head and

tattoos, in exchange for access and information. Some may say I shouldn't have to, but doing what needs to be done IS who I am.

Discovery Questions

- Can you adjust how others perceive you to access new resources? Is it how you communicate via email, phone, or in person?
- Where is the line of a tweak vs changing who you are at your core?
- Why does it matter to stay true to who you are?

Frontera Guatemalteca

La frontera de Guatemala era aún más humilde y pequeña que la de México. Nos bajábamos para estirar las piernas y mientras papá iba a la casilla de aduana nosotros fuimos corriendo al baño.

Me di la vuelta, pues sentía que alguien me iba siguiendo, pero no vi a nadie. Al lavarme las manos, vi en el espejo pasar una sombra corriendo, pero de nuevo, no vi a nadie. Fui a buscarle a Noe alguna merienda y era cada vez más obvio que alguien me iba siguiendo, pero era como una sombra que se desaparecía cada vez que me daba la vuelta. Escuchaba los pasos que me seguían, pero con las preocupaciones de la frontera decidí que era mi imaginación y que no pasaba nada.

Papá me mandó a quedarme cuidando la troca en lo que los demás terminaban sus asuntos. Al fin un poco de silencio para sacar un libro de mi mochila, en donde vivían mis amadas heroínas o mi diario de dibujos y pensamientos, ¡BOOM! Salté de mi asiento al

Guatemalan Border

The Guatemalan border was smaller and more humble than the Mexican one. We all unloaded to stretch our legs, and while Papi went to the booths to get our paperwork situated, we all ran to relieve ourselves to the bathrooms.

I turned around because it felt like someone was following me, but I didn't see anyone. After washing my hands in the restroom sink, I saw a passing shadow, but when I looked again, I still didn't see anyone. I went in search of snacks for Noe, and I became increasingly aware that someone was following me, but it was a disappearing shadow. I could hear the footsteps nearby, but with the worries of being in a border town, I decided it was only my imagination and that nothing was really happening.

Papi sent me to sit in the car to watch over it and our belongings while everyone completed their errands. At last, some peace and quiet where I could enjoy a book from my backpack where my

ver que un muchacho sucio y deforme me golpeaba el vidrio y del susto no podía distinguir si reía o lloraba. Intenté ir corriendo a la puerta del otro lado y rápidamente se dio la vuelta y ahora estaba golpeando el otro vidrio, con la misma cara de angustia o felicidad, no podía descifrarlo. Me atormentaba el sentimiento de no poder salir a ayudarlo. Y así mismo como apareció se fue corriendo cuando llegó Pablo a decirle que se fuera de ahí. Después de pasar el susto Pablo se burlaba de mí diciéndome que había dejado a mi novio en la frontera.

beloved heroines resided or my diary of thoughts and drawings. BOOM! I jumped out of my seat when I saw a deformed and dirty young man banging on the window nearest me, and from fear, I couldn't discern if he cried or laughed. I quickly scurried to the opposing door to try to open it, but he arrived with the same face of anguish or joy that I could not decipher. I was tormented by my inability to step out to help him. Then, just as he appeared, he vanished when Pablo arrived to demand that he go away. After the fear passed us, Pablo teased about the heartbroken boyfriend I'd left at the border.

12

WAIT OUT THE DREAD

*"Every time I visit my accountant I feel like
I may be more and more Republican."*
-An anonymous entrepreneur, definitely not the successful Chef

still had everyday bills and an imaginary goal that everyone knew I wanted to create. The masculine clothing store I'd had an event at allowed me to cut hair and shave on my days off to keep chipping away towards saving. Nick, a world-renowned Chef and prominent Dallas restaurateur, was a regular at the store. As I polished the beautiful antique barber chair, I introduced myself, my services, and the dream behind why I was barbering in the store window. He was kind enough to partake in a haircut and shave. He shared his journey and how he was busy in the throes of entrepreneurship and creativity. We coiffed his locks into a tapered, professionally subtle mohawk. He blessed me with great advice and encouragement through the dreadful waiting each time he stopped in.

I had regular mentorship meetings with Jefferson to go over my business plan with actual numbers. We would refine and polish the plan as he saw my determination to achieve my vision. Adopting the mindset of "fake it till you make it" was helpful during lease negotiations because any bank I approached wanted to see real numbers.

Jefferson and I developed a point system that helped me decide on significant issues for the business. One of the biggest ones was location.

Deep Ellum was art-fueled and creative, and its cultural history was rich with grit and stories. Addison was central, had a nightlife, and was one of the only non-dry counties back in the day, which accounted for the popularity of Beltline Road and commerce.

Potential students lived a particular lifestyle while my ideal barbering clients lived in alternate neighborhoods. How could I find a balance between both?

Deep Ellum takes people back to the early days in Chicago. From the outside, it gives the look that promotes tradition. I wanted to generate the rebirth of the straight razor shave experience. The location had exposed raw brick, and the old look would transport clients to a slower era. How do we create a mob hangout style with the cigars while acceptance, hope, and encouragement are on the menu daily?

Our point system considered the following:
- location
- accessibility
- build-out costs
- my commute
- community

The rules to the point system meant that once it was decided, we didn't have the conversation on that topic again.

I contacted a realtor to assist me with pricing for what could be the Academy. The places he kept drawing me to were those small, hidden office spaces that are not on a main road, tucked away, and would never attract drive-by or walk-by traffic.

I would drive around and search for my own information in locations that seemed promising or at least fun to work in. I would send the realtor addresses explaining I needed a space that was within budget and that also offered inspiration and connection to some sort of community. An angry, seething email was finally received from him informing me that I would never meet my goal, that I would never find the location I was dreaming of, and that it simply did not exist within my budget. It felt pretty condemning and confusing.

Throughout multiple commercial properties in Deep Ellum, most of them sported the trademark of a signature yellow sign. Their presence seemed everywhere, but I opted to call them anyway. The most aggravating part of it was getting a straight answer.

How much was the square footage? How many locations did they have in the Deep Ellum area? What type of businesses did they usually represent in that area? All of these lead to more questions from them. The voice on the phone sounded like a younger wanna-be guitar player who was a little too full of himself.

At one point, he finally said, "We want to poll our potential clients before we share any information. For example, how much do you want to pay a month?"

It pissed me off so much that I responded to him, "One dollar. My ideal price point is one dollar a month for rent!"

Needless to say, after finally having met him, my instincts were correct. He was a wanna-be guitar player, and maybe that's why he was so frustrated at his day job. I did not want to do business with that level of negativity, never escaping the fear, doubt, and confusion behind turning my dream into reality.

I used physical exercise to stay sane through this process and ran regularly. During my runs through Deep Ellum and Downtown, I would make mental notes of the vacant locations with other small businesses nearby that would complement what I was trying to create.

Jefferson and my point system yielded Deep Ellum as our ideal location. Yes, it was gritty and less busy than Addison in the daytime, but it won the most points.

Eventually, on my run, I came across a small storefront that was for lease. It used to house Deep Ellum radio, and it was next to a dilapidated hydroponic store and a black dark-covered facade. Still, I wasn't sure what business it conducted.

Upon researching who the building owners were, I learned that they owned multiple commercial buildings that housed small businesses in the area for over 40 years. They were family-owned, and they cared about the community. I hoped that if those other smaller businesses had made it work, maybe I would qualify as well.

I could never have imagined that we would eventually be a brand sought after to the point of infringement as far away as Dubai.

Noe was working with a very talented hair artist in Downtown Dallas. He had built a gorgeous marble-filled salon with high ceilings and the promise of becoming a busy fixture in the Dallas salon realm.

He had wonderful training and talent, and he believed in education and recruited an A-Team. He'd even gone as far as doing construction in it himself, and it was splendid. The problem was that he'd spent over a year without being able to function as a salon. The city wouldn't change the "use" of the space into retail from it having been a fur coat sales shop for decades... in Texas.

He and I would meet at Buzzbrews to talk life and shop. I felt so badly for him because entrepreneurship was tough enough as it was before adding a year of no revenue on top of everything. He was dedicated, driven, and kind enough to share what he had been through with me. This lesson made me verify many things about potential locations that I had not been privy to. I would make mistakes, but not the same mistake that had cost him dearly.

The landlord of the potential location gave me the information, and it seemed it could be realistic. With Jefferson's suggestion, I called a few architects to quote me on the blueprints since we would need them to get accurate bids for the different trades required for a buildout.

I had never interviewed for an architect, and I scheduled six at different times on the same day. By the third one I interviewed, I got the hang of it.

By the end of that day, I knew if I moved forward, I wanted to work with a laid-back gentleman, Mike, who still drew his plans by hand. Mike had the calmness of experience with the kindness of an old friend. I needed both.

His speed and experience meant that a team of younger architects tried to keep up and digitize what he drew with a pencil.

Once the plans were delivered, I could scout out general contractors and have the different trades bid. All of this information helped me to feel confident in the numbers in my business plan.

My friend Michelle, who had helped in my fundraising process, called me one day and told me she had a dream of the academy. "We were inside sitting on the floor having Chinese food," she encouraged me to keep hope. We both laughed because there wasn't any Chinese food near our loft or side of town, but we just accepted the idea and vowed to do it if we ever opened. I could only hope.

Polishing and refining the plan into reality while pursuing the project as if I had the funding helped me to materialize it despite the obstacles and naysayers.

I needed divine intervention to maintain hope.

Diamonds In The Rough

- Encouragement and life experience shared by actual entrepreneurs breathed life into continued hope in a way nothing I could read had.
- A phone call from an invested friend helped soothe the dreadful waiting.

Discovery Questions

- Meditate or focus on fellow entrepreneurs' struggles, and instead of thinking, "That could never happen to me," assume that it could. How can you avoid a similar pitfall?
- What are the next tangible steps you could take by assuming that funding is arriving soon?

Guatemala

Al fin entramos a Guatemala y qué hermosura nos esperaba. Al ofrecerle una propina a un soldado guatemalteco, nos respondió que sabía que habíamos salido de México y que él ya tenía su sueldo. Nunca sabremos si fue un gesto de amistad de parte de nuestros amigos de caravana, pero se nos hacía un sueño hecho realidad.

Guatemala estaba radiante, jamás he vuelto a ver un verdor parecido, ni la cantidad de pájaros coloridos volando entre las cortinas de hierba y árboles. La ventana no me bastaba y la velocidad de la troca no me dejaba absorber toda esa extraordinaria belleza como hubiera querido. Tucanes de mil colores nos llenaban la mirada de ilusión en vida y los quetzales eran una realidad y nos iban saludando mientras nos pasaban volando por el lado.

A Noe ya se le empezaba a terminar la leche en polvo y por la prisa que llevábamos, Pablo se bajó en un puestecito a averiguar el precio y los tipos de leche para reponer la res-

Guatemala

At last, we entered Guatemala, and what beauty awaited us. After offering a tip to a Guatemalan soldier, he mentioned knowing we had spent days dealing with Mexican militia and explained that he already had his pay for his job. We will never know if it was a friendship wish from our caravanning Guatemalan friends, but it seemed a dream come true to have arrived.

Guatemala was radiant, and I had never seen such vibrant green nor the multitude of colorful birds flying through the curtains of herbs and trees. The car window did not suffice in width nor the speed of the Montero to allow me to take in the extraordinary beauty as I would have loved to. Toucans of vibrant colors filled our eyes with illusion in the flesh, and Quetzales were real since they greeted us by flying by.

The milk supply for baby Noe was starting to run low, and with the rush we were in, Pablo was allowed to run inside a small kiosk to see about brands and milk prices. He came back,

erva. Se acercó corriendo a la ventana a decirle a mami, "hay leche LaLa, Nini y de otra." Todos confusos nos quedamos viéndole y soltamos una gran risa. Papi se bajó y averiguó que las marcas de leche eran distintas a las de Dallas.

El hotel colorido con vidrios encima de la pared de cemento que lo rodeaba fue donde nos establecimos para seguridad y descanso esa noche pero era imposible dormir tarde. La mera idea que nuestras Tias y Nanitas nos esperaban con esmero y delicias eran mas que lo podríamos imaginar.

running up to Mami's window, and proceeded to butcher the name brands, which caused laughter from the adults. Papi went inside instead and quickly learned that the brands in Dallas are different from Central America.

The colorful motel, with broken shards of glass installed on the top of the concrete fence, was where we were all crammed for safety, but it was impossible to sleep in. The sheer idea that our Tias and Nanitas awaited us with affection and delicacies was more than we could think because we were so close to El Salvador.

13.

KEEP AN EYE OUT FOR ANGELS AMONG US

"We are the only major city in America not founded on a port or navigable river. What others needed the ocean to accomplish, -we did with sweat."
-Brick wall at Dot's Hop House, Deep Ellum, TX

Based on my religious upbringing, I have always believed in angels. Surely there are the glorious, magnificent ones painted on the ceilings of architectural works of art. While I have not consciously met one of those, I have met plenty in human form. I prefer my angels to be accessible and closer than heaven.

I was getting closer to creating the place that would be Blade Craft, and I knew that I would make mistakes. I solely focused on not making the same mistakes that had caused dear friends so much pain.

Mike, the architect, was going to join me at the good ole permitting office in Oak Cliff, TX, to ensure that the use of the space allowed what we needed not to repeat my buddy's leasing disaster and heartache. We continued to polish and refine to report back to Jefferson. Jefferson and I had a budding friendship; he liked teaching, and I loved learning.

I wondered if Jefferson would be my partner or stay my mentor. He certainly checked off the list of things Mr. Law said my ideal partner would.

Parking at the city permitting building, your typical city oatmeal tan brick on the outside, buzzed with lines full of colorful people, tickets, and forms on the inside.

Dressed as responsible-looking as I could muster in a teal A-Line dress, with ivory heels and dominated bleached blonde locks into submissive retro curls, I walked in, took a number, and waited. Holding my plans and purse in my lap, I settled in to take in my surroundings.

There was a door through which numbers went; they emerged with forms and then lined up at the cashier to pay. In and out were suited City Employees who oversaw the many constructions and developments of all types of businesses all over town.

The guy next to me was hyperventilating, the contractor with dirty jeans in front of me looked pissed off, and again I'd found myself in a boys club not exactly invited. If the Hyperventilator would cry or yell, I couldn't tell, but if he came in regularly and felt that way, I was scared. Would he explode?

"Ma'am, may I see your plans," called a tan suit.

Oh god, please don't let it be me. There was no way he was talking to me.

"Ma'am, yes, you."

I stared at him wide-eyed.

I blinked.

I panicked. Now I understood the hyperventilating. I was hyperventilating on the inside.

"Not yet. I'm waiting for my architect, who is arriving any moment now," I blinked and responded, flustered but matter-of-factly.

He had a stern, hurried expression and wasn't comfortable with hesitations.

"I can look over what you have so far while we wait for him," he directed.

"I really must wait for him," I countered.

He spun, and in the door, he disappeared.

Phew. I had staved off Tan Suit for a few moments, at least. I didn't speak blueprint, and I sure hadn't learned a city permitting accent.

My phone buzzed. A text from a dear client turned friend stating that Tan Suit would be able to help.

Huh? What?… How did anyone know I was here?

All he said was to ask for Tan Suit once the architect arrived. Mike arrived, and I mentioned everything to him, and he coolly suggested we go along with it.

We did.

The use of the space?

Perfect.

While in many cases, it's easier to ask for forgiveness than permission, this time, a friendship angel arrived to help things through. From desk to desk, we hopped, and where there were questions or hesitations, Tan Suit had a response.

Stamp of Approval. New Desk. Stamp. Next Desk. Stamp.

Going confidently in the direction of my dream yielded a Certificate of Occupancy for a space I had not yet signed a lease on. Neither Mike nor I knew how, but we were sure the space was right. I was happy to have someone witness the road opening for me after so many doors closed.

Cost analysis for signage and permitting seemed elusive to me, and I called Wes for his guidance. He referred me to a furniture maker to obtain a suggestion, and I followed up.

The office was small and full of handmade details on the tables, lamps, and even the restroom. The Carpenter was covered in sawdust but friendly, and I explained that I needed a quote for a sign.

I explained what I was trying to accomplish as the end goal and that I was still in the pricing phase. He asked if he could see the plans in my hands.

Carpenter said, "Let me understand. You have not signed a lease, but you are obtaining all the permitting and plans in advance?"

I nodded.

" You also already have a CO?" he asked again, like it was a big deal.

I nodded.

Grinning from ear to ear in his carpenter gear, he said, "You're crazy. The trades are going to eat you alive. I'm in."

Visiting the highest office for building also helped me filter and find other like-minded professionals to keep pushing forward.

These two green lights were getting me hyped for what would be. It wasn't a NO today!

Diamonds In The Rough

- Paying a visit to the highest office I could think of at this stage yielded unimagined results!

- My upbringing in a small Pentecostal church in West
  Dallas shaped my sense of connection, comfort in the
  uncomfortable, and belief in more than what we can see.
  I wouldn't say that I consider myself a religious person.
  Still, I will never forget the instructions and suggestions
  from the biblical parables.

Discovery Questions

- What is the highest office for the top three important
  aspects of your business?
- Do you have plans, services, or items that can be purified
  by running them through scrutiny before you feel like
  you are ready? (without jeopardizing your project, of
  course)

Preguntas A Papi

¿Cuántas preguntas habrá tenido que aguantar mi pobre padrecito durante todo el viaje?

"Papi, usted dice que son las llantas que dan vuelta pero yo no le creo. Es el piso que nos pasa como un Treadmill."

"Mire, si yo fuese abrir la puerta con el Montero andando y pongo el pie en el piso, el pie seguiría."

"¿Pero usted cómo sabe papá?"

"¡Ay Lilly, que risa! Pues yo soy el que manejo y sé por experiencia que no es así. Y acuérdate que las llantas las veo yo y se acaban al igual que el gas" se reía.

Questions For Papi

How many questions did Papi have to endure through the whole trip?

"Papi, you keep telling me that the wheels are turning while we are in the car, but I don't believe you. I think the floor moves past like a treadmill."

"Look, if I open the door and place my foot on the ground, it would get pulled back from under."

"But how do you know Papi?" we asked.

"Oh, Lilly, what a joke! Because I am the one driving and have life experience, to lets me know it is the car that goes forward, not the treadmill concept. Also, I see the tires, and they run out, as does the gas," he laughed.

14.

GREEN MEANS GO

Then one day, Mari, the crowdfunding contact, reached out. "I wanted to call you and give you the good news instead of emailing. You have been approved for the amount you need, and we can close next week."

What? Huh? The bank saw what was presented, and they said ok? The first person I called was Randy—my voice of reason, pep talker, and all-around cheerleader.

I couldn't understand if I still wanted or needed a partner and if obtaining the startup capital would be enough. I couldn't understand why I'd been approved for the loan right as I had found such a promising potential partner. Sure, he and I had not discussed if he would become my partner, but he sure behaved like one.

"Options are always a good thing, and there isn't any harm in considering a hybrid version! I always knew you could do it! Of all the people I have worked with, I knew you'd make it happen!"

Randy observing the process to the green light of the loan made it seem all that more real, and I was elated!

The following person I called was Jefferson. "Helluva job! Well done! Go close!" he beamed.

Here I was again. Another project full of emotions I had never felt before. My dream seemed tangible, and it was not only acknowledged but proven to be full of potential by a bank. People who math-ed for a living felt my business plan was solid and sustainable enough that they'd fund me?!

Of course, I had to fetch a few more bones, but those were quickly attained. Feeling unusually flustered, I called Jefferson to try to talk through the disarray.

"One thing that will make you a lot less nervous is to pretend that they are nervous and make them feel comfortable about the whole thing and forget about you. They have to sign new leases all the time, and most of the time, it will not work out. In this case, it will, and you and I know you were born for this. Thank them for the effort and help them make sure that it is right and make this the most pleasant lease signing experience THEY ever have and forget about you.

"We will take care of you later, so make this about them, and all your anxiety will go away. Just one good lease and loan and let the rest of life take care of itself because you never know. Forget about yourself and make this pleasant for them and call me and tell me they had a great experience and that you got the photos.

"Do not overdo your workout for anxiety; instead, remove your ego from this and do a reasonable workout. You will do great. If something goes wrong, then we can always do it again on Monday! Chill. Or, in your case, I guess chili. I will be waiting for your call. Also, even though I am CEO, it helps me to pretend that I work for my partner, and I kind of do. So, as your partner, you work for me. So do it and report back. That way, your ego is out of it. No ego, no fear!" he shared.

As much as I knew better, I woke up with all the nerves. Yesterday, I'd met up with the architect and MEP engineer to tie up some loose ends and had forgotten the blueprints at home. It hadn't helped that it was raining and the highways in DFW were full. I could have cried when I arrived without the plans. I talked myself out of thinking it was a bad omen.

Instead, I resolved myself to get as good a workout as ever. After running me through her CrossFit workout, I invited my friend to join me at the closing for moral support. Today, she had one job: to take pictures of my signing and to not dare ask one question on any of the thousand pages of signatures I was to sign or its contents in that there was absolutely nothing that could or would be changed. I promised her ice cream afterward. She was so excited!!!!

Back at the loft in Deep Ellum, I teased my blonde hair to the highest of heights. After all, "the higher the hair, the closer to God." The long black legs of a backless romper would ensure that I was the happiest, prettiest closer of any loan she would ever have.

Upon arriving, Mari said, "Girl!! You look gorgeous! But are you sure you want this loan? It's A LOT of money, you know?"

"Where do I sign?!"

"You're crazy," she confirmed.

The process began, and it was final after a paper cut or two. I was handed a large cardboard check, and the pictures were snapped.

We then immediately sped off to meet the landlord at a coffee shop to sign the lease. He had gone through all the last-minute requests for the bank with me and was so excited to see me there. With him was his youngest daughter. She was four years old, sweet, spoiled, and loved. I spent most of my time conversing with her about whether a cake pop was more delicious than a chocolate chip cookie. He handed me the keys after we signed, and I took a picture squatting beside the little one to send to Jefferson, fulfilling the stops of my homework assignment.

My vision fogged over when he responded that my Dad was surely in heaven, proud of his own little girl that day. We went and had ice cream. Of course, we took a picture.

Experiencing a green light to build the world's best barber academy was an incredibly uplifting experience. Mari calling to inform me of the approval of my small business loan was a thrill unlike any other!

While green means go, the 90-day deadline to spend the build-out funding had begun. Negotiating with trades to ensure the academy was a reality was a new skill to be honed.

Diamonds In The Rough

- The slightest attention to ensuring that others are cared for can really remove the spotlight from your fears.
- The fear of attaining what you have worked so hard to achieve can be overwhelming, but having a clear vision of your why helps ground you.

Discovery Questions

- What does a green light look like for you?
- What will you do if everything goes "right"?
- Do you have a recurring hit list of green lights?
- How did you celebrate your last green light?

Llegamos

Cruzamos el puente Manuel José Arce, el cuál une a Guatemala y El Salvador, justo pasado el anochecer."Gracias Maestro." El proceso en la aduana era sencillo pues todos los adultos eran nativos.

El mapa nunca nos falló. El sol sale para todos.

Empezamos a ver los camiones llenos de vendedores de todas las edades ofreciendo a galillo abierto frutas y postres.

"¡Agua! ¡Agua y juuuuuugoooo! ¡Agua! ¡Agua y juuuuuuugoooo!"

"¡Mangos tiernos! ¡Se venden mangos tiernos!"

"¡Empanadas! ¿Cuántas le damos?"

Todo era fresco y todo era a mano.

Si les pedías una bolsita de manguitos tiernos, le ponían un poquito de sal y limón fresco. Si querías empanadas, las servían con una bolsita de salsita con curtido al instante. Los olores eran fascinantes y Mami me recordaba que, "El sol sale para todos mi niña."

We Arrive

At last, we crossed the bridge Manuel Jose Arce, which unites Guatemala, and our long-awaited El Salvador just passed nightfall. The dealings at the border were quick and easy since it was my parents' native land. "Thank you, Maestro," Papi prayed in gratitude.

The map never failed us. The sun rises for all of us.

In the morning, we started to see all the soniferous buses full of vendors of all ages offering their fruits and pastries at full yell.

"Water! Water and juuuuuice! Water! Water and juuuuuice!

"Fresh Mangos! We've got some fresh Mangos!"

"Empanadas! How many do we get you?"

Everything was fresh, and everything was handmade. When you ordered the fresh mangos, they placed salt and a slice of fresh lime. If you wanted empanadas, they served them with a small bag of fresh salsa and instantly produced slaw. The scents were intoxicating,

Llevaban delantales de colores pastel con bolsitas escondidas de más obvias, con moñitos y encajes. El uniforme de un buen vendedor ambulante empieza con aseo y termina con ser amable y eficaz. En cada parada de bus se subían y se bajaban antes que se fuese el conductor.

A Mami siempre le ha gustado usar sus vestidos de colores alegres y largos y para mí mejor, siempre era fácil encontrarla aunque estuviera en medio de mucha gente. A mami nunca le ha faltado la confianza para ponerse lo que le gusta.

"Mira, estas sandalias sí son de cuero bueno," me decía al encontrar zapatos abiertos. Siempre me ha fascinado el olor que tienen las tiendas de zapatos de piel.

and Mami reminded me, "The sun rises for all of us, my girl."

They wore hand-embroidered aprons of pastel color with hidden pockets from the obvious ones, with bows and detailing. A successful mobile salesperson's uniform always begins with impeccable hygiene and ends with efficient kindness. They got on and off at each bus stop without disrupting the driver yet still addressing the passengers.

Mami always enjoyed wearing long dresses full of joyful colors, which was great because I could always find her in a crowd. Mami never has lacked the confidence to wear what she wanted to.

"Look, these sandals are made of great quality leather," she pointed out at the nearest market when she found elegant open shoes. I have always enjoyed the smell of leather goods stores.

15.

DARE TO BE OUTRAGEOUS WHEN NECESSARY

*On negotiating: "Meet in the middle. Always leave
something on the table so that the other person feels
good about the project. You never want to work with
someone who feels taken advantage of."*
-Jefferson

The gunshot to start the blindfolded marathon seemed to have gone off finally. It was a frenzy to see how I could complete the build-out and begin making revenue before I had to start paying the bank and the landlord soon to follow. The neighbor next to our new build had been told that his lease wouldn't be renewed in January. His rants and temper tantrums demonstrated that he wasn't a fan of the decision and we were somehow to blame.

The wall connecting housed beautiful and intricate glass bongs, pipes, and fixtures on his side. Our dilemma was finding out if the wall was salvageable and if it had a shiplap that we could recycle.

Frustrated with not having found a contractor, I mentioned to Mami that I needed someone to remove the sheetrock to see what was underneath. She met me there to assess it and offered to have one of her tree service guys help. I left her the key and headed to work.

When I arrived at the end of the day, she had personally removed the sheetrock ever so carefully to the extent of her arm's reach. Not a single piece of glass fell on the opposite side of the wall at the neighbor's store.

When I asked her why she hadn't received help, the day laborers didn't arrive, and she wanted to personally ensure the neighbor wasn't upset. The project should not be delayed behind something so simple as seeing what was under there. I couldn't believe it.

There are times when drive, or shall I call it a devil-like stubbornness, possess me, and I have but to think on that wall to understand. We may not know the answer, but we aren't afraid to get our hands dirty.

Growing up as a day laborer for odd-end jobs for my father, I had an abstract understanding of the process of a build-out. His absence in my life felt extra heavy on these days in that if he were here, I could just call him, and he would have solved all of it.

Heather of the textbooks was one of the first phone calls I made to place an order for ten sets of everything we discussed. Once the books arrived, they sat in my loft for months until the build-out was completed, but they were there!

The stuff we see on the outside of a building is only the makeup of what lies beneath. The mechanical, electrical, and plumbing are the organs, sinew, and blood that allow the outside facade to flourish.

When hiring for these jobs, I saw that the people executing them are as different as the jobs they produce. Architects were confident. The plumbers were comfortable with slop. The electricians were concise. The painters were proud. The engineers were know-it-alls.

Working 40 hours a week to provide for myself and overseeing the build-out while keeping costs down, it seemed only rational that we would polish and reseal the concrete floors ourselves to save on cost and feel some control of its progress. Pablo thought that we could accomplish it. He referred me to his neighbor Mike, who also dabbled in AC work to help. His Texan accent only I understood, but he joined Noe and me on a few of the projects to make it happen. We rented machines from Home Depot, got face masks, and went off.

"Easy peasy!" said Noe, standing at six feet tall and more than capable. Yet the task was quickly getting out of hand. The problem wasn't lassoing the buffer machines, nor the clouds of concrete dust, but the side effects of the now dust bowl we had created. We couldn't contain it. Our hands blistered, and despite years of sweeping hair, nothing has compared to the pain of sweeping concrete.

Establishing something that will stand past the shelf life of concrete weighs more than I had known. Would I be able to see it through?

In the Bible, we'd read about work. My parents talked about picking cotton, selling food in the sweltering sun, fishing, and holding various jobs. They'd warned about how easy we had it in comparison to others. They were all right.

The vision was something I held on to through those exciting seasons. Instead of feeling overwhelmed, I was exhilarated every day, being the last one there at night and the first to arrive in the mornings.

Here was MY shot at MY dream, and I would give it my all.

Our pissed-off glass neighbor had a tangible reason now to despise us because his store was a victim of the dust. Oh, how he hated us!

My blonde hair had a more "concretey" tone to it, and I feared that water would reactivate it in the shower, but thankfully that isn't how it works. The only real problem was trying to hold clippers in blistered hands and exhausted arms.

Carpenter and I had kept in touch, and he arrived with a surprise. The antique clippers from Corsicana would shake many more hands since, through reincarnation, they had now been transformed into door handles. They would comfortably welcome the new barbers on their journey and the guests in their experience.

Sometimes, it's up to you to make the door handle that opens the door you've longed to walk through.

If something is important enough, you will figure out how to do it yourself, from discovery, polishing concrete, or creating the door you need to open.

Appreciating opportunities to progress forward can be a salve when things don't go our way.

Diamonds In The Rough

- Mami taking matters into her own hands by removing sheetrock when the workers didn't show is a visual representation of how I overcame many obstacles.

- The carpenter creating the door handle from the manual clippers added a symbolic touch to the door.

Discovery Questions

- What is an example of needing to do something outrageous to pursue your dreams?

Soldados

El aliento de la naturaleza trae consigo un olor a cenizas y la frescura de las hierbas y el olor a tierra mojada. Como todos los demás niños de allí, nos pasábamos los días jugando a las escondidas pero también ayudamos a ordeñar las vacas, a limpiar elotes y a desgranar el maíz.

En una de esas tardes en las que salíamos a explorar, pasando el árbol de tamarindo nos fijamos que había unos soldados con metralletas acostados boca abajo; y Pablo y yo no pudimos contener la curiosidad, nos acercamos a ellos lentamente y le preguntamos qué miraban, a los soldados les cayó en gracia que dos niños no les tuvieran miedo, nos mandaron a irnos a casa pero yo les recordé que era la propiedad de mi abuelita y que pues, ¿qué hacían ahí? Al llegar a casa emocionados a contar nuestra historia nos regañaron, nos explicaron lo que era la guerrilla y que aquí los policías no eran igual a los de los Estados, que siempre debíamos tener cuidado porque las per-

Soldiers

The breath of nature brought the aroma of ash along with the freshness of herbs and freshly wet earth. Like the rest of the children, we passed our time with games like hide and seek and assisting with chores such as milking cows and shucking and shelling corn.

One afternoon, we went off to wander and explore. Passing the tamarind tree, we noticed soldiers with heavy machine guns lying face down on the ground. Pablo and I couldn't contain our curiosity, and we approached them slowly and quietly to ask them what they were observing. The soldiers found amusement in that we weren't afraid of them. Still, they sent us home to our parents, expressing there were dangers to be met when unattended. We reminded them they were on our Grandparents' land and asked why they were there.

We returned home excited to relive our adventure but were scolded and told our views of heroic police officers in the States might not apply

sonas con metralletas pueden ser malas. Pero al menos ese día, los soldados se fueron y se dieron cuenta que en el lugar donde estaban, no estaban bien escondidos.

to these soldiers, who could be bad people. At least for that day, we were safe, and the soldiers left, realizing they weren't well hidden.

16.

ACT WHEN BAD THINGS HAPPEN

Rule 1: Stand up straight with your shoulders back.
-Dr. Jordan Peterson

H e got teary-eyed about the project. "Herman, porfavor, call me Herman." Rough working hands with the recognizable paint splatter spots on the nail beds grasped the wrinkled invoice book. He wore the standard Latin carpenter's uniform consisting of a tucked-in undershirt into worn-in jeans with a belt.

The tears were heartfelt after my explanation of my dream turned to calling, and how if my father were here, I wouldn't need anyone.

We agreed on a bid for him to act as the General Contractor instead of me faking it. We shook hands and began. If only things could be that easy.

Things go wrong, but you can and will find a way to create something that wasn't there.

The uneasiness began when, after my morning and evening stops in between work, I noticed he wasn't listening. There were clear instructions in trying to preserve the grittiness and integrity of the building.

There is a beautiful murky metal framed window that allows natural light in. After having lived in my loft with 30-foot high ceilings with windows as the majority of one of my walls, I would not live without the natural light.

After informing Herman of this, his workers put an AC drain through it. I addressed it, and he fixed it, only to have an exhaust vent pushed through it the following day. After each reminder, it would be fixed, only to be ignored again.

He also was adamant about me not being in the building during inspections since he "knew" the inspectors "for years."

Then, there were the excess draws for cash. Obviously, to start a project, revenue is needed for materials, labor, and permitting.

After the third uncomfortable conversation, I confirmed with his staff that his attention was on another project, and so were the funds.

I struggled to swallow after the giant knot formed in my chest—equal parts anger, sadness, and betrayal.

But why? Why was I so emotional? He was my elder. I was the client. Two conflicting principles were at war internally. In my work, the client is King, and I thrive on getting it right. I'll happily problem-solve, be fully present, and further educate myself to constantly improve for each interaction.

In my heart, elders are King, and I'm honored to engage. It isn't just my culture but my upbringing in that small church. Elders extended such kindness to Mami upon arriving in Dallas, and she still remembers their advice on mundane things like a recipe or how to protect herself in an accident. I found myself in a tug-of-war on values.

To make matters worse, Christmas Eve was my last day as a full-time barber at a real job with a clear boss and clients. The front desk was pissed because I was booked until 6 pm, but my clients were all loyal to the last possible second. They wished me the best, and the tears flowed with some when they weren't sure they'd ever see me again. My last day was here to support myself in the only way I had known how up to this point.

On Christmas Eve, Herman texted me, stating he needed cash because his son-in-law had something bad happen to him.

My response: "I'm sorry that happened to your son-in-law, and I hope he recovers soon."

Send.

"I will only give you cash as the progress points in our contract are met."

Send.

The last in-person interaction with him was on the day of the last payment. He decided he'd add extra expenses, which I hadn't approved. We parted ways with a letter from my attorney. Years later, rumor had it he lost his license to work in charge. Turned out he did know the inspectors "for years," after all.

While bad things happen, attention to detail and clarifying your values will clarify your communication. The devil is in the details, especially when wading in the full brunt of the unknown.

Diamonds In The Rough

- Having clear values will help your decision-making process.

- Keeping important agreements and communications in writing via email or text helps to clarify each party's intention and roles.
- Despite my discomfort in challenging an elder and conflicting values of respect, the urgent need to finish the project on time was a greater concern.

Discovery Questions
- When was the last time you had conflicting values?
- Did you find that you can also honor both through critical thinking?

Los Dias Pasan

Durante el día, las tías se ocupaban de las delicias y los niños hacíamos varios quehaceres. Por la mañana nos íbamos tras el falso por las vacas para llevarlas al potrero y del potrero las llevábamos a tomar agua al río. Por la tarde nos daban pailas de frijoles para surtir y si no maíz para desgranar.

Mi abuelita Carmen por las tardes nos daba cafecito y no sé qué tenía ese café, pero siempre nos tumbaba del sueño. Recuerdo un día que mi abuelito Chico me pidió que le ayudara a poner un arete en la nariz al chancho para que dejara de escarbar y cuando el chanchito comenzó a chillar, entonces chille yo más. Me fui corriendo a contarle a Papi pues, ¿qué culpa tenía el chanchito de querer escarbar?

Days Pass

During the day, our Tias occupied themselves in making delicacies, and the children kept up helping wherever we could. In the morning, we were allowed to go behind the barbed wire fence where the cattle were kept, and we took them to pasture and to drink water at the river. In the evenings, we received pails of beans to sort or more corn to shell.

Abuelita Carmen would give us homegrown fresh coffee, and I have no idea what was in it, but it knocked us out into restful sleep. Abuelito Chico asked for my help one day in holding down the cutest piglet, and then he pierced a metal loop in his snout so that he wouldn't dig up the vegetables anymore. The piggy squealed and cried, but I cried more as I released my end and ran to tell Papi about the injustice. What fault had the piglet to want to smell things closely?

17.

PROTECT YOUR FRIENDSHIPS

"In time, people will always find out that
they were taken advantage of."
-Jerry White

Jefferson and I decided to formalize our partnership agreement. "Contracts protect friendships," was another of his sayings, and I needed help. I even had a shower installed in case I couldn't afford a home and had to live at the Academy until it took off. The 90-day deadline was around the corner with both my sanity and funds depleting. We met at a cupcake shop and signed our Company Agreement per Mr. Law's blessing.

Jefferson informed me that I needed to hire an assistant because even Mormons go out in pairs, and that must be based on some sort of data.

I took on the task and really started after any build-out detail and finishing touches I could physically push through.

Some moments in life feel surreal, like a movie in which you are living in the flesh.

It may be because Papi was a carpenter that doors, ladders, and windows are images that recurrently speak to me.

I was searching for a unique doorway, and Jefferson suggested I ask Pablo to make it. Pablo told me to find the wood I liked and that he'd give it his best shot. I found a beautiful rosewood that posed the challenge of changing in color with the sun's light when he'd go inside for water while working on it.

In Lewisville, an extremely talented stained glass window maker could create the Blade Craft logo in uniquely cut pieces for the opening in the door that Pablo had designed. Once installed, its size, function, and beauty would symbolize his support.

One of my regulars had missed the Lilly on Location events and donated all the light fixtures for my academy! He pulled up, personally dropped them off, and enjoyed the dusty tour showcasing what would be. His generosity helped immensely.

Papi had always shown me what he found beautiful in builds.

"Hecho a mano," he would say.

"Made by hand."

"Mira, estos si saben."

"Look, these know what they're doing," he would say as he explained that what was beautiful almost always took extra effort and craftsmanship. Curved walls, circular windows, archways, and intricate faucets caused headaches for others, but it was a welcome slowdown for him. It called his attention.

Enter the porthole.

With my phobia of swimming and the idea of a submarine as distant as space travel in my mind's eye, porthole windows seemed like the perfect add-on to the design of the suites.

I already knew hurried girls rounding corners to get their clients on time meant bruised thighs and long days. The outside walls of the suites must have rounded corners to prevent that, and we designed makeshift porthole windows in those walls. When a build begins, windows and light fixtures tend to be the last things installed to prevent breakage.

To remain sane, I demanded that my suite be the first thing completed to ensure that I could still serve my guests while the delays of buildout, city, and state might occur.

I had my regulars to care for and help me cope with the chaos.

During this season, my assistant would come to speak to me through the window, bring lattes, or simply make eye contact since the design meant that I could see most of the shop through tricks of the mirrors.

The porthole would need to open and close on a swivel, and Carpenter scratched his head but made it happen.

I envisioned that decision serving me well throughout the years in checking in with students as they built their independence in my suite. I could test their nerves by tapping them on the shoulder when they focused on a facial and would be able to maintain open communication.

My new partnership was encouraging and insightful in that someone as well-established as him was willing to bet on me. I needed all the encouragement I could get to stay afloat for all the motion sickness to come.

Diamonds In The Rough

- Contracts protect friendships.
- Sometimes, you can even enjoy tangible proof of other's love and belief for you.

Discovery Questions

- The porthole was a real addition to my build-out. However, what is another perspective you can try to see your project in a different light?
- Is there something you should be working on but haven't buckled down to try?

Tia Chunga

Papi tenía una tía que vivía en frente de abuela Carmen, Tía Chunga, que siempre nos llamaba a escondidas para que fuéramos a su casita, desde que entraba encendía una vela para poder ver en la oscuridad, allí rebuscaba en sus bolsas hasta que encontraba una anona madura y lista para comer que había preservado fuera de temporada quién sabe cómo.

Tía Chunga era sorda pero podía leer los labios y hablaba en susurros. Nos contaba historias de su juventud, mientras Papi hasta se tomaba una siesta en su hamaca. Frecuentemente le enviaba cartas a Papi para saludarlo y una vez le regaló una foto de ella firmada en la parte de atrás que recuerdo, Papi siempre llevaba en su cartera, junto a la de nosotros, sus hijos.

Por las tardes salíamos a jugar fútbol o canicas debajo del palo de Tamarindo, el dulce de tamarindo era fresco y delicioso.

Los adultos se ocupaban de barrer, lavar la ropa, secarla,

Tia Chunga

Papi had an auntie who lived in the house facing Abuelita's front door, Tia Chunga, who always called us over in mysterious whispers in hiding for us to go over to her house. As we entered, she lit a candle so we could see, and she searched in her plastic bags until a fruit called anona emerged, which she had acquired out of season somehow.

Tia Chunga was deaf, but she could read lips, and spoke in continual over-enunciated whispers. She would tell us stories of her youth while Papi napped in her hammock. Papi would receive letters and postcards from her in the States saying hi to him, and he even carried a signed photograph of her in his wallet behind our picture.

In the afternoons, more soccer or marbles under the tamarind tree yielding delicious treats, the centerpiece of Abuelito's yard.

Adults were lame and swept or did laundry, which they'd run to bring in from the clothesline when it rained.

correr a recogerla cuando se venía la lluvia desprevenida.

La pobreza de nuestra gente a veces me parece curiosa y me hace preguntarme, ¿qué es en realidad la pobreza? Si el río cada día nos trae agua y el candil nos ofrece luz, si la fuerza física del trabajo de campo nos da salud. La pobreza aparenta ser la ropa o los zapatos nuevos que tanto disfrutamos, pero ellos viven felices, sin deudas.

La educación se mide en el respeto que le brindamos a la familia y el ser una persona digna y para la buena higiene personal hay todo un manual de trucos, las hojas para sacar la mugre de las uñas, la sal para cepillarse los dientes, la hierba buena para ayudar con el mal aliento.

The perceived poverty of our people seemed curious to me and had me asking myself what poverty actually is. The river brought us cold mountain water daily, the candles offered light, and the physical strength of our labor brought us health. Poverty might seem apparent without new clothes or shoes, but they lived debt-free and at peace.

Education was measured in the respect we offered our family members. Being a decent human and having good personal hygiene came with many fun tricks. Leaves could be used to remove grime underneath the nails, salt could scrub your teeth, and spearmint was available for added freshness.

18

HURRY UP AND WAIT

"There is always room for the one person
that is willing to do it right."
-Jefferson

Spring in Deep Ellum is beautiful. The trees bloom, and the sun really enlivens the murals and textures. We finally began giving tours to potential new students and sharing more on social media about who we were and what we were trying to do. To my surprise, the students were more interested in the longer, more robust Barbering program, and I couldn't believe it!

The build-out was finally complete except for minimal details, and we had passed all of the inspections with the city. We had started giving tours but weren't sure of a start date since the State wasn't getting us a response on our curricula approval to be able to train new barbers.

It isn't that I am a certified genius, but certainly, I am not a procrastinator. When creating the curricula, I didn't know what I was doing, but I had so many examples of what I didn't want.

Week-by-week schedules became day-by-day schedules that next became hour-by-hour breakdowns. I had called the hard-working ladies at the state department to outline their punch list and timeline.

These calls consisted of long hold times, impatient personnel, and finally assumed clarity.

"Once you apply for a barber school license and submit your packet, it takes about a week and a half to get processed."

The package, license, and check were certified speed mailed off the second the physical facilities were up to specs. After receiving the alert that it was delivered, I gave them a week and a half to ring again.

"Oh NO honey… it's going to be AWHILE…"

"What do you mean AWHILE specifically? Days? Weeks? Months? When I called before, they wouldn't accept my package until a week and a half prior to it needing to be done?"

I waited. I emailed. No response. Two more weeks.

Yellow lights can prove helpful if intentional with the time.

"You'll know when I know ASAP the happy date for your first day of class!" was the repetitive response for when prospective students could start classes. It was exasperating in that rent, bills, the bank, and the cost of a buildout were also realities that were daily antagonists.

A dream isn't dreamy if you can't make payroll.

I called the state again. The same woman on the other line seemed annoyed, frazzled, and frankly put off that I had to keep ever too excitedly checking in. The bottom of her emails were signed, Betty.

Have you ever had the experience of interacting with someone and imagining that they are a character from a cartoon or movie you've seen? I envisioned the character behind the desk of Monsters, Inc., who, in the end, is a good guy but seems to enjoy sticking it to the little guy. Roz is the name of the character, and she has the typical cat eyeglasses, the look of "I'll catch your flaws," and, of course, the lipstick.

As this new vision filled my mind, I realized that this person despised human interaction as much as I enjoyed it, and nothing would irk her more than me in the flesh. So I came up with one of those bad, but hopefully good for me, ideas.

Heather of the textbook company was phoning to see if I'd be interested in a video and photo shoot for the shave chapters in the next edition of the international textbook of barbering.

They were looking to update their material, and I was the exact opposite of what had previously been the standard, and she felt I was perfect. That dream gig helped cover part of the rent for the academy while I was still trying to hunt down some clarity on my opening. Here was the universe throwing me a life preserve when I needed it.

I called to redeem my Chinese food voucher and enjoyed it on the floor, just as Michelle had imagined it! I wanted to inhale the elements of this reality with her and keep reminding myself that it was really real.

I dressed in my Sunday best and drove to the State Capital with flowers, a balloon, and Blade Craft Swag. I headed to the address at the bottom of some of her emails. I needed to find Betty and understand the hold-up or how I could improve on what I'd delivered.

Upon arrival, it was obvious that I had NOT made an appointment and that visitors weren't exactly a thing. This fact surprised me in that I always assumed that it would feel like the Driver's License office and that they saw as many citizens.

I smiled from ear to ear and could hardly contain my excitement to understand even more of the process. I waited in the cafeteria that looked and smelled like what I imagine the 70's did and placed my journal on the table.

Betty appeared in the doorway, frazzled and kind—the glasses, the nails, and far from understanding why I was there… in person.

I couldn't decide if she despised my energy of two coffees or the questions outlined on both sides of my journal that I wanted clarity on. Her feigned smile let me know to move swiftly.

My gifts were not accepted "cause, you know, bribes." What did that mean?!

"Austin is one of my favorite places to visit!" The awkward visit was over, and I was returning to Dallas.

Red light.

I placed my headphones in, got on a smooth highway, and called Jefferson. I updated him on my failed attempt. This place just felt gross. It wasn't green or red or even yellow. We were idling, and I no longer had my full-time job, nor did we have control.

"You need to take a vacation," he said.

"What the hell?! I can't do that. We have spent the money. We completed the build-out. I have an assistant. I have tours, and the academy still can't enroll students. We can't even plan our Grand Opening." I was confused.

"If you had a boss who, every time you worked really hard to accomplish something, you went to alert them that the task was done, and they immediately gave you something else to do, you'd say they were a shit boss. You have accomplished a lot even though you aren't open. Take four days away somewhere and do not touch a curriculum, or market, or anything to do with this project," he insisted.

I conceded, but I disagreed. I got off the phone call and played tunes instead. I focused on the road ahead and couldn't understand how leaving for four days could help advance things.

Then my car started slowing down. I began to panic until I realized I was just out of gas. I hadn't heard any of the alerts because of my headphones. I pulled over on the service road, called my brothers, and looked up destinations while I waited. Turns out Jefferson might have been right. I needed some time away.

I awoke the next day to a 7 a.m. email from the state informing me that somehow my curricula application had made it to the top of the stack.

Green means go. Pedal to the metal baby!

I was living a dream transformed into a reality! People were touring, moved by the passion in our program, and genuinely interested in becoming Blade Craft Barber Academy students. A vendor even put me up for a job opportunity that was really helpful, and even when my trip to Austin seemed null, it turned out to be a valuable experience for me.

Diamonds In The Rough

- Sometimes, even when I don't agree, it helps to attempt the suggestion of a friend.
- Put the key in the ignition and go talk to the person you feel is the closest to the obstacle you are dealing with.
- A full circle closes because it was first put in motion.

Discovery Questions

- When was the last time you experienced a full-circle moment of an effort you made?
- When was the last time you attempted advice from someone you respected that you weren't fully sold on but came to understand while executing it?

El Llano

Después de unas semanas, cuando finalmente nos olvidamos del cansancio del viaje, nos volvimos a montar en el Montero para irnos de viaje con los papás de Mami. Unos de los mandados en estar en su país era la Sastra, el dentista, y el mercado para mis papas.

El oro servia para cubrir los dientes picados por los años sobrevividos en agua cual su potabilidad sigue questionable.

La pobreza experimentada por mis padres incluía falta a recursos a la educación, pero jamas en se aseados.

La basura quemada la convertían en jabón, y los mascones crecían en los arboles. El perfume no falta con hojitas de flores combinadas con aceite. Lo que faltara se reponía con amor, cariño, y deseo de trabajar para salir adelante.

La niña Elisa era una anciana que tenía un perico que recitaba las oraciones del Padre Nuestro y Ave María, siempre nos esperaba con charamuscas y con las masitas frescas que recibía cada día.

El Llano

After a few weeks, when we could let go of the exhaustion of the road, we loaded back up into the Montero to head over to Mami's side of the family. On the way in, we stopped at the tailor, the dentist, and the markets for errands for my parents.

Broken gold jewelry was recycled to cover chipped or broken teeth from years of questionable water and lack of access to dental work.

The poverty experienced by my parents in their childhood resulted in less education but never in being dirty or messy.

Trash was burned and converted into a brown soap, and loofahs grew on trees from local foliage. Anything missing was supplemented through love, affection, and a desire to work to progress forward.

Niña Elisa was an elderly woman who had the most well-trained parrot who would recite prayers like Our Father and Holy Mary, and she always awaited company even without warning, greeting us with charamuscas and fresh masa hand-

Cuando llegamos al llano de Los Patos fue la primera persona que visitamos, Mami quería que viera lo grande que estábamos, con su sonrisa de oro brillando y brillando.

made tortillas. When we arrived at the Llano de Los Patos, she was the first person we stopped to see. Mami wanted her to see how big we'd all grown, and her gold smile shined through and through.

19.

CELEBRATE THE WINS

As luck would have it, the dream job in the textbook landed on the same week of the Grand Opening. I saw it as a lucky omen because my excitement in welcoming every-one to Blade Craft Barber Academy with a start date behind it was more than I could hold in my limbs.

The culmination of this moment was a symphony out of disparate and inanimate concepts coinciding just so to create and give birth to something that wasn't there.

I was in New York on set, loving every second of the barbering experience. My hands were purple from the cold, and I did air squats to maintain energy between takes. I strived to excel at every request of the Director and somehow convey the mesmerizing quality that I loved about straight razor shaving to the future barber who would be watching. I mean, why is a straight razor shave so damn exceptional?

How many times have you realized that something done for you by somebody else is so much better? The sandwich made by a mother tastes so much better despite having had access to the same ingredients. The coffee poured by someone else hits differently. A flower picked just for you smells even sweeter.

Shaving: as mundane as second nature as brushing your teeth or combing your hair, it can become a portal into a faraway place of luxury, masculine sexiness, and slumber. Rituals become so because of connection. I tried to give it my all.

During one of the meal breaks, I called Mami.

"I'm freaking out! I'm trying to do my best, but I am so concerned about the Grand Opening this weekend and any details I may be missing."

"What is there to worry about? I arrive with the tacos at 1. What more do you need?"

"You're right, Mami. It will all be great."

Family and friends attended the grand opening to celebrate and enjoy live salsa music, cigar rollers, fellowship, laughter, and connection.

New students starting their journey in the first class danced along with friends I had known as a young girl! Surrounded by loved ones, a dear friend, Dr. Rick Rigsby, led a Champagne Dedication where I broke a bottle on a wall in the alley for good luck. Of course, it took a few times, but there were tacos.

I felt exposed when the butcher paper was finally removed from the windows. Anyone could look in. Anyone could engage.

This ship was finally on open water in motion to receive the calm or storms to come, porthole windows and all.

I'd never imagined the sensations of the experiences, adventures, or connections to arrive inside. I simply had the Academy on the horizon. The Academy was now the vessel in which I would pursue the horizon.

It was Christmas in May, and our excitement was only matched by the students embarking on their new journey. They had received their smocks and toolkits, and we had even shaved balloons! Noe was a student in the first class as well, and it was the end of our very first Initiation Day. He and I could hardly believe that we'd pulled it off!! Each student had left with a smile on their face, and each moment was ingrained in my heart in the dream materializing into reality. They were so happy! We were so happy! Could this be real life!?!

As we were cleaning up for the day, Noe happened to notice a gentleman looking in our window. Noe walked out, invited him in, and gave him a tour. A couple with him caught me up. Apparently, he was a famous hairdresser overseas and had just won the American Crew's All-Star World Champion Award. His salon was in Spain, and he loved our facility. We wished each other luck!

A few months later, Heather had an industry event to attend in Dallas, and through hugs and tears, I got to give her a tour of Blade Craft Barber Academy in the flesh.

While enjoying BBQ at the Pecan Lodge, I tried to express the hope our calls had meant for me during that time prior, but it was something to experience. I was convinced that what I was experiencing was so special, and I was dedicated to staying in my lane.

Blade Craft Barber Academy was real. I find it challenging to put into words what the moment felt like—experiencing something so beautiful in this realm that I'd seen only in a dream almost hurt.

I wish I could tell you that after opening Blade Craft, graduating students, and building a clientele, everything remained as rose-colored as these moments.

Diamonds In The Rough

- Translating my thoughts when calling Mami helps me achieve clarity and mutual understanding.
- Mami providing her tacos for the event brings me comfort through the fear of experiencing such an awaited moment.
- Rituals are what we make them.

Discovery Questions

- How do you celebrate your wins?
- How big does a win have to be to merit attention or reflection?

Un Regreso

Después de tanto cuidar y atender al famoso Montero, finalmente le llegó la oportunidad a Papi de presumir la fuerza del motor del Montero en el que tanto había trabajado. En un viaje saliendo del Llano, nos encontramos con un lechero ambulante al que se le había atorado el camión en el lodazal y con el peso que llevaba se hundía cada vez más; y papi que siempre estaba dispuesto a prestar una mano a quien lo necesitara, decidió ayudar al señor, después de darle varias vueltas y analizar la situación, acomodó el Montero con cadenas y cuerdas para sacar el gran camión de su situación, antes de que se le echara a perder la crema, leche y todo lo demás que llevaba cargado cuando se deshiciera todo el hielo.

Después de atar todas las cadenas a la troca, ¡Vroom, vroom! Fue todo un éxito y el Montero logró sacar el camión del lodo y así rapidito partió el camión lechero a su destino. Pablo brinco de alegría y todos gritamos de gozo al ver

A Return

After all of the attention and care that Papi had put into the famous Montero, he finally got the opportunity to show off the power of the motor he had worked so hard to install. On the trip leaving El Llano, we found a milk truck stuck in the road on the thick, soggy mud, and under the added weight of all it carried, it sunk deeper into the peanut butter-like muck. Papi, who was forever available to lend a helping hand to anyone in need, stopped to offer assistance to the driver. After getting out to walk the circumference of the area to analyze the situation, he attached the Montero to the truck with a series of ropes and chains to create a weird pulley system to get the grand truck out of its situation before the cream, milk, and everything else it contained got ruined once the ice melted.

Once everything was safely fastened on the milk truck - VROOM, VROOM! It was a total success, and the Montero was strong enough to unstick the large truck out of the mud.

que si funcionó. Papi abrazo a Mami orgulloso al ver que todo su trabajo había valido la pena, mucho más de lo que se había imaginado, "ya ven que la Montero no falla" dijo sonriendo.

And it quickly hopped on the road and went about its route. Pablo jumped for joy, and we all cheered to see that it had worked. Papi hugged Mami, proud to see that all his hard work had been worth the fuss, even more than he could have ever imagined, "you see that the Montero never fails, " he grinned.

20.

Check the Rearview Mirror

*"Never, ever give up. You're never too old
to chase your dreams. It looks like a solitary sport,
but really it's a team effort."*
-Diana Nyad

"**I**f you build it, they will come!" they say. Bullshit.

If you build it, work really hard on it, sit outside while smoking a cigar, and an elderly man walks by with his adult grandchildren, he may compliment your hat. You may trade hats with him and share a good laugh! So many random stories of connection like this have fed my dream and fueled my journey. However, these stories don't easily translate to sales or the revenue required to feed the insatiable toddler that is your business. Toddlers are messy, filterless, and self engulfed.

I don't know what to tell you. Fire in the belly. Passion. Conviction. People can tell if you really are where you wish you were. They are attracted to that because it's what everyone wishes they enjoyed in their respective lives.

If they don't live it, they are genuinely inspired and happy as shit that you do. THAT is what they support. Living a dream not only makes the dreamer joyful but also those who witness it too.

The product is secondary to your purpose.

Storytelling is only wonderful if there is someone to hear it. Connection can only happen within the circle of the sender and receiver. Physical touch is exceptionally restorative and recharging. Dress for the woman at the bank, treat everyone like a customer, or bring all team members a coffee in the morning.

The Blade Craft Barber Academy Family keeps growing! At the time of this publication, well over 40% of our graduates own their own businesses, and the rest primarily work for a small business that positively impacts their community. Our team strives daily to model what the barber can do in their community through activism, community service initiatives, and integrity.

We carry our brand with pride, many to the point of tattooing it. Many Salons and Barbershops hold job openings for our graduates. We have been invited to the World's Largest Reality Show on Entrepreneurship, The Blox, as a judge. We work with businesses for speaking engagements and provide technical training. That isn't just Lilly on Location. We are committed to superior service as a team, and the future is bright!

Get lean or die isn't just a fitness idiom. In a small business, cash flow must be watched over futuristically, not just in the immediate moment. My staff is counting on a fun, empowering, actively encouraging, and high-level environment. Our students expect to be challenged through compassion and nurturing while using the best products and having access to the best clients on earth. Our neighborhood needs us to walk the walk to protect our way of life, art, culture, and freedoms. To remain badass, we have to be the brightest light that you can possibly envision in order to obtain the slightest flicker that you'll need to keep going one day.

The energy at Blade Craft Barber Academy is like nowhere on earth. However, just like a soul has a body, the tangible facade, plumbing, lighting, barber chairs, and the roof is a temporary house for its current version. Just like a body needs yoga, fruits, veggies, tacos, and a doctor, the building does fucked up shit sometimes that causes me to wonder why I love lather instead of fire hoses.

We have but the consciousness of THIS life. Actual presence is a practice. When a person is in front of you, it's a true sign of connection to be there in that precise moment.

I often get asked if I'm excited about an event in the future. I receive puzzled looks when responding that I am excited about THIS moment—the one at hand. I'm excited about my client, who will be walking in any minute, or the class I am about to lead.

It's been my experience that, for some reason, our society always celebrates romantic love over other expressions of it.

Friendship love is underrated and has been a healing salve for my soul throughout many facets of my life. Friendship love has nurtured me, encouraged me, and helped me stay on this side of reality.

I consider my relationship with my brother a form of friendship love. I also feel blessed with my decades-long clients' version of friendship love.

One of my greatest desires on this earth is to have successfully been a good friend, not in the way that I define it, but in the way that someone needs it. I truly believe that we are on this earth for each other, and any ideology that claims we can do it all alone, I think, is shit.

The now is permanent—the present matters.

Building something doesn't ensure buy-in. Human connection does. Hindsight is 20/20, but it can help in deciding the future.

Diamonds In The Rough

- The continual work of maintaining any relationship applies to a storefront.
- Purpose matters more in the long run than the product.
- Friendship love can always be cultivated.

Discovery Questions

- How does your product align with your purpose?
- If your product involves a storefront, have you considered the daily, weekly, and monthly upkeep and resources required to shine?
- Have you ever had a memory creep up, a scent, or a song remind you of a friend you haven't heard from in a long time?

Espumosos

Llegó el día de mi cumple años y tía Emilia nos iba a consentir con sus postres que había aprendido hacer trabajando con unos Padres en la capital. En el primer puestecito nos introdujo los espumosos, que estoy convencida que vienen directamente de la cocina de los ángeles del cielo, son unos postrecitos de color pastel que se deshacen tan pronto tocan la boca.

Mientras nosotros disfrutábamos de todas las delicias, nos asegurábamos de licuarle a Noe todo lo que se pudiese licuar y le poníamos trocitos de frutas en la boquita, así no se perdía de nada, qué bebé más amado, nunca le faltó cariño.

Después de la fiesta, nos fuimos todos a pasear a la playa de Las Tunas cerca de donde vivía la gente de mamá. Nos metimos en la parte de atrás de un camión grande y ahí íbamos todos los primos y familia meciéndonos todo el camino, cuando llegamos a donde mi nanita en el Cantón Llano de los Patos, convenci-

Pavlova

The day of my birthday had arrived, and Tia Emilia was spoiling us with some of the desserts she had learned to make working at a monastery waiting on priests in the Capital. At the first pastry shop we visited, she introduced us to beautiful pavlova cookies that I am convinced are baked in heaven's kitchen by the most loving angels. They are pastel-colored, softer than cake, and dissolve almost as soon as you eat them.

While we appreciated all the deserts, we would mash them up to share with Noe so that he would enjoy every delicious savory thing. We placed tiny pieces of sweetened fruit for him to eat, and he was the most loved baby I have ever known in that he was never missing affection or attention.

After the party, we all went to a beach called Las Tunas, close to Mami's family. We all loaded up into the back of a large open shipping truck, and all of us cousins swayed and laughed in the wind on the bumpy roads. We swung into

mos a la familia para que nos acompañaran también.

Cuando llegamos a la playa probamos las minutas, que son raspadas de hielo a la cual le ponen miel de tamarindo o piña. El señor del puestecito andante llevaba churros, gaseosas y de todo lo rico, picoso y ácido que al paladar de niño caen como anillo al dedo. Y mami, que es amante a todas las frutas, nos dejaba comer hasta saciarnos.

La risa de Mami se escuchaba desde el mar y se veía radiante bajo el sol por su sonrisa de felicidad. Papi se esmeraba en hacerla reír y siempre le atinaba.

La arena, las olas, el sol y el mar daban la ilusión de que el día duraría por siempre. Cuando nos cansamos de bañarnos y jugar en el mar, fuimos a las chozitas que estaban al ladito de la playa, que tenían toallas y hamacas para relajarnos. Ahí probamos los curiles, que es un tipo de sopa helada y fresca de color negro que se hace al momento que se encarga y es perfecta para refrescar la calentura que causa el mar.

el Llano de Los Patos and convinced some of those relatives to join us.

Once arriving at the ocean, we enjoyed handmade sno cones sweetened with a thick fresh tamarind or pineapple syrup. The man who owned the mobile kiosk also sold chips, sodas, and every sour, sweet, or craving-inducing delicacy you could imagine that, for a child's taste buds, leaves nothing to yearn for.

Mami's laughter could be heard from the ocean, and she radiated under the sun's rays because of her love-filled smile. Papi aimed to make her laugh and hit his mark more often than not.

The sand, waves, sun, and ocean gave the illusion that the day would last forever. When we were tired of swimming and playing in the ocean, we could go over to the palm tree-covered huts close by with towels and hammocks to relax in. We tried curiles, a cold black soup with mussel-like protein made once ordered and cooled the feverish symptoms of too much sun.

At dusk, once satisfied and rested, we found our truck

Al atardecer, ya satisfechos y descansados salimos a buscar al chofer para volver a casa y justo en ese momento empezó a llover y con la piel quemada del sol, nos pegamos todos juntitos y nos fuimos tambaleando por las calles maltratadas, todos agarrados para no caernos.

driver to head back home, and of course, the rain began as soon as we started on the road. We clung to each other to escape the lashings of the cold rain on our sun burnt skin, holding on for dear life on the winding roads and slippery surfaces.

21.

DALE GAS

"Nil nisi cruce."
"Nothing without suffering."
- Victorian motto

The brown butcher paper is covering the windows from the inside. Threats of looting from desperation, anger, and fear are coupled with promises of overdoses and suicides.

We cannot sit outside and trade hats with passersby while smoking a cigar, and we dare not hug a neighbor.

The em-ocean waves are as fierce as they are calm, and the current seems to have swept everything from underneath. There should be outrage. The asphyxiation is trifold.

We are muzzled everywhere we go with face masks. The quarantine is house arrest. We are prohibited from making a living.

Fear, however, is the most deadly and dangerous source of asphyxia.

Fear of being asymptomatic without testing.

Fear of losing our livelihoods.

Fear of unemployment.

Fear of government control.

Fear for our Black Brethren who have suffered far too long.

Fear of losing our loved ones.

George Floyd's words, "I can't breathe," carry too heavy a weight. The loss of his life in the hands of the police we trust was unnecessary. We were not created to destroy our communities and connections with our fellow man. However, we have the experience of something created that once wasn't there. It having been done once means that it can be done again.

Hello, unwelcome friend. There you are again. The waiting. The unknown. Uncertainty.

When embarking on a journey to create something that isn't there, the waiting is more painful than a no.

All is not lost today. The sun seeps through the corner of the butcher paper and increases as the last of it is removed. I keep the paranoia to welcome others in and the unanswered questions that linger every breathing second at bay.

We have a tour.

"El sol sale para todos," recuerdo que me dijo Mami. "The sun rises for all of us," I remember Mami said.

Humming.... today hummed. It was the days after a full moon. I asked, and I received. I asked Deep Ellum for models for a unique technique, and guest after guest arrived on time.

The students were so ready. Apparently, the instruction was understandable. The team was each soaring in their part of the shop, and it was beautifully cohesive. The minutes passed, the energy was in our grasp, and it felt like play all day!

Texts rolled in, confirming that the day had been incredible. Shears had been cutting, razors were shaving, and students learned what fulfillment of good work could be.

I reminded each of us to hold on to today. I reminded myself that this was only my hope not too long ago. The hope of what could be was followed by the agony of the work to be done.

Today, there is the gratitude of the re-actualization, and we arrive tomorrow only to begin again.

"Lo hecho una ves fácil se puede volver hacer," said Mami. "Dale gas."

"What is done once is easy to do again. Give it gas."

Diamonds In The Rough

- The unknown is actually a familiar place.
- Do not lose hope.

Discovery Questions

- How do you keep sight of constant hope?
- If you keep constant reminders of goals achieved, are those in visual or audible forms?

Palo Santo

Después de haber disfrutado de la compañía, la comida y las experiencias vividas con nuestra familia, había llegado el momento de despedirnos y regresar a nuestro hogar en Dallas. Papi decidió acercar el Montero al Río y lavarlo a mano. En una cubeta hizo jabón y con trapos usados empezó a enjabonarla. Cuando terminó de lavarla, empezamos a enjuagar con el agua.

El agua fresca nos refrescaba al bajar por los cerros. Las gotas de agua translúcidas corrían por los vidrios cubriendo todo.

¿Cómo íbamos a imaginarnos ese día que la corriente de lágrimas por venir serían inmensurables? ¿Qué la tristeza y el llanto nos nublarían la visión durante las décadas siguientes?

Las maletas, los postres, los antojos, todo guardado dentro de la Montero mientras abrazábamos a nuestros seres queridos y les decíamos, "Salud." Papi abrazó a su

Holy Tree

After thoroughly enjoying our family's company, food, and experiences, it was time to say goodbye so that we could return to Dallas.

Papi decided to drive the truck up to the river and give it a good hand washing. He made soapy water in a pail, and with used fabric, he began to suds it. After washing it thoroughly, we began to rinse it.

The water traveled down the mountains and hills and refreshed us. Translucent water droplets ran down the windows and traveled past the mirrors covering it all.

How could we have known that the current of our tears to come would be immeasurable? Sadness and grief would cloud our vision for decades to follow.

Our luggage, desserts, and cravings had all been loaded onto the Montero, and we hugged our loved ones with the traditional greeting "Salud."

Papi hugged his mother and received her blessing.

A journey done once can be done again in reverse.

Madre, recibió su bendición y nos despedimos.

Papi abrazaba a su Madre, recibía su bendición, y se despedía.

Un viaje hecho una vez, se puede volver a cumplir en reverso.

Bajamos los cerros, pasamos San Francisquito, y nos encaminamos en la calle abierta.

Al llegar a la aduana nos moríamos de la risa al leer un rótulo en un árbol que decía "No orinar."

Y que de los demás palos? Y que de todo lo demás? Los niños y los hombres se orinaban en donde quisiesen menos en ese santo palo.

We descended from the hills, passed San Francisquito, and entrusted ourselves to the open road.

Once we arrived at El Salvadoran customs on the border, we cracked up laughing at a sign attached to a tree in the center of the plaza that read, "Do not urinate here."

What of all the other trees? What of everything else? Men and boys could pee anywhere except on the forbidden holy tree.

A Nightmare Becomes Reality

It was the Summer of 2008, and Papi wanted us to join him for a Quinceñera in El Salvador. He and Mami had been divorced awhile, and we all knew that it weighed on him, but things were as they were. We had a wonderful time immersed in the scents, connections, and meals! He stuck to his vow of not trying to dig wells or patch up roofs while we were there and attempted to enjoy a vacation for once in his life.

We could not have known how the summer trip would be some of our most cherished memories with him. Back in Dallas, on November 13, 2008, on the foggiest morning since the 1920s, my father was coming home overserved and inebriated from a bar at 5:30 a.m.

He got on I-20, going the wrong way into oncoming traffic. He collided head-on with an 18-wheeler. He lost his life instantly.

He was driving the Montero.

I can barely recall the call communicating the accident, but the rage to prove it was a lie I still feel to this day. I have tear-filled memories of driving to Noe's high school. He was only 14 years old at the time. My baby brother came in with the bounce in his step he's always had - so full of joy. He mistakenly assumed I was there to take him to lunch and have him skip the rest of his day since I was accustomed to doing so, only to inform him that my lifelong nightmare was now a reality.

The veil of grief has blurred over 18 months of my life. I recall us overdoing every holiday immediately after his loss. I can't remember the details, only the effort to find relief from the pain.

I remember parking my car at the accident site and walking along the indestructible concrete barriers. The speeding sound of intense traffic was trying to solve something in my mind. I recall mindless drives to the cemetery to sit by his grave. I remember trying to uncover ways to numb the loss, but there were none. There was a detachment.

Mami, Pablo, the kids, and my Noe all felt the grief in waves.

The translucent tears escape past our defenses and will often creep up to be wiped away. There are still times when they become torrential, so we must believe we will be together again.

Epilogue

Experience is like a well-worn piece of clothing. Just because you are familiar with it doesn't mean it isn't helpful or useful to someone else. You may wear it casually, but someone going through a similar situation for the first time could use your insight, just like our impoverished cousins could use the clothing items.

In creating the academy, I now had free rein to design opportunities that gave back to causes that are dear to me. We offer the Opportunities Solutions Program to connect those needing tuition assistance with options to obtain their dream of a career in connection through barbering at Blade Craft Barber Academy.

Epílogo

La experiencia es como una camisa favorita que por ser conocida no significa que no le sería útil a alguien más. Tu te la pones casualmente pero para alguien que esté pasando por tu misma experiencia con duda y miedo por primera vez, tu punto de vista le es útil como la ropa usada le era a nuestros primitos.

En crear algo que no estaba allí tenía rienda suelta para brindar oportunidades a las causas tan cerca de mi ser. Ofrecemos el Opportunities Solutions Program para conectar a quienes necesitan asistencia financiera para alcanzar su sueño de una carrera en conexión con la barbería en Blade Craft Barber Academy.

About the Author

Based in Deep Ellum, Texas, **Lilly Benitez** is the esteemed Founder and Director of Blade Craft Barber Academy. Globally recognized as a leading barber trailblazer, Lilly has deep ties to giants in textbook publishing and tool manufacturing. As the Brand Ambassador for Jatai Feather Razor and a published expert for Barbering Textbooks, she stands as a trusted authority in her field, inspiring many with her unique insights.

Lilly is also deeply committed to her community. She holds a chair at the Deep Ellum Foundation Association and actively advocates for the barbering industry, monitoring legislation that could impact it. She champions the craft for its transformative power - from offering financial freedom to enhancing neighborhoods through skilled professionals.

When she's not busy barbering, Lilly cherishes moments with her husband, pets, family, and friends, often accompanied by a fine cigar.

Connect with Lilly
www.bladecraftbarber.com/blade-lilly
Email: info@bladecraftbarber.com
Call the Academy: 214.434.1476

About the Publisher

Reader Advanced reimagines how books are advanced, published and sold. Scan QR code to Learn More: